THE ONLY SOUNDS WE MAKE

ALSO BY LEE ZACHARIAS

Helping Muriel Make it Through the Night
Lessons
At Random

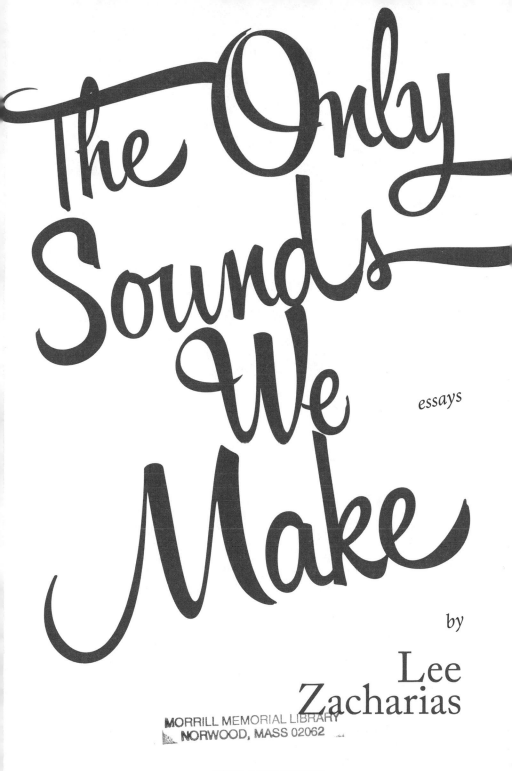

The Only Sounds We Make

essays

by

Lee Zacharias

HUB CITY PRESS
SPARTANBURG, SC

814
Zacharias

First printing: May 2014
Cover and Book Design: Meg Reid
Proofreader: Sally Johnson, Jill McBurney
Copyeditor: Jan Scalisi
Printed in Saline, MI, by McNaughton & Gunn Inc.
Cover Photo © Patrick Joust

Library of Congress Cataloging-in-Publication Data

Zacharias, Lee.
[Essays. Selections]
The only sounds we make / Lee Zacharias.
     pages cm
ISBN 978-1-938235-00-9 (pbk. : alk. paper)—ISBN 978-1-938235-01-6 (ebook)
1. Zacharias, Lee. I. Title.
PS3576.A18A6 2014
814'.54—dc23
[B]
     2013032680

186 West Main St.
Spartanburg, SC 29306
1.864.577.9349

for Max

CONTENTS

—

IN THE GARDEN OF THE WORD

—

I.

THE WEATHER IS SWEET. In this town that has, like so many others, a Market Street, the median is planted with trees called weeping cherries; they are weeping the palest pink blossoms. In my yard daffodils and forsythia are already fading into azaleas and dogwoods, whose uncurling green fists promise the spectacular white lace of spring. Even the sidewalk is fragrant with the earth warming beneath it. I have opened a window in my study, for on this afternoon I am inside, writing a novel.

I am imagining another spring day, decades ago, a day on which 25,000 people gathered on the grassy slope behind the Washington Monument under a bright blue dome of sky with the warmth of the sun soaking into their shoulders. They are protesting the Vietnam War, but it is 1965, the war is young, and on such a day neither I nor the character I have singled out from that crowd can summon anger. She cannot know of the bitterness to come, the mood of protest turning from hope to blind fury. The scene is already written, but I surprise myself by adding these lines: "It is not possible to believe in evil on a perfect spring afternoon, and in its absence, one places faith not in the tangle of conditions between, but in good. It is in this error that we come to be moral."

2.

BUT WHAT DO I MEAN, exactly? Pronouncements are as final to a scene as the tonic note to the musical phrase, though the composer is under no obligation to explain his structure, for its meaning is contained in its sound. My obligation is to imply the clear and impalpable thought in the palpable word.

I'm not sure that those two sentences do the job, which will fall to all the words that have lesser pretensions, the *he saids*, *she saids*, and little flashes of gesture and detail that leave most of what they should say unspoken. But I, who have the obligation to know every word that isn't said, am thinking about what it is like to be human.

What do I mean by "this error"?

Something like this: If to be human is to be fallible, it is precisely because no other creature makes the mistake of assuming itself to be moral. Nature admits of design, but not of motive. In search of one, we claim an identity apart, which is both our grandeur and our sorrow, for we die in the company of dust, but live in the crux of good and evil.

3.

I AM WRITING THIS NOVEL by day, for I am on leave from my job, and at night I discover a luxury I haven't known for years. I close *Curious George*, call Daddy, who sings "Hail to the Redskins" far better than I do, kiss my small son good night, and climb into my bed, free to read anything I want. It is an ornate iron affair, my bed, picked up for ten dollars from an antique shop beside an Arkansas highway fifteen years ago, and it requires four fat pillows to keep its medallions from printing their whorls on my spine. But imagine—four fat pillows, a quilt worn soft drawn up beneath my arms, the hood of yellow light, the rose-colored walls, Steiglitz's *Flatiron* in its dusky mist of gum bichromate evoking the comforting sound of wheels on wet pavement, my husband's closet open and spilling ties. And on my bedside table whatever book I choose. I am a child again, propped up on the sofa, sick and home from school. My husband is kind—he brings me coffee soothed with milk; he is a reader too, and he understands that reading is, in the act itself, a sensory delight.

It is easy to forget that when you read for a living: stories in search of publication, student manuscripts, the hundred pages you must teach tomorrow and have no time to savor. One finds pleasure in the best of these words too, but the act is not the same: I find some other place to do it: the desk where I write checks (never the one where I write fiction), the wing chair, a couch, the breakfast table. To reject a story, write a comment, or annotate an anthology in my bed is as unthinkable as sleeping on the stove or slicing onions in the bathtub. It is the place of sex and dreams; one may read happily in such a setting, but conduct business never.

4.

MY APPETITE IN READING is for narrative, my attraction to stories, any story, so instinctive that I cannot remember when it began. My mother claims to have toilet-trained me by threatening never to read to me again, and yet, once I was able to read to myself and the Little Golden Books of preschool were all packed away, I recall growing up in a house without books, save a few condensed novels from *Reader's Digest* and a paperback edition of *Peyton Place* my mother kept hidden beneath a clean white towel in the linen closet. My father worked double shifts at an oil refinery; my mother kept house, shopped for bargains, and sewed my dresses, strewing the living room with patterns, straight pins, and gaudy tufts of thread. We had a new television, and that was our frill.

It was by most counts, I think, a fairly ordinary childhood, given the time and place and class, far too mundane and intellectually impoverished for the standards of any child I know today. My own son is spoiled with the books and excursions and consideration of his questions that I wish I had had. Television is to him a VCR with a Disney classic or British actors playing Ratty, Moley, and Mr. Toad. What could my parents know of how I would look back? If they were children of the Depression, I was a child of their affluence. They were pioneers of the postwar cliché, astonished by the luck that work could bring them: a small house, hands that fed their mouths, and at day's end an hour of Arthur Godfrey or Milton Berle.

I went to the sort of schools where English meant another dreary day of linking verbs that the kids in the back row never seemed to master, in the sort of town where library cards were stamped *adult* or *child* and the librarian called your mother if you tried to check out *Jane Eyre* instead of the little orange biographies of *Mary Mapes Dodge Jolly Girl* or *Eli Whitney, Boy Mechanic*. I adored Maud Hart Lovelace, whose Betsy, Tacy, and Tib grew up with me. (Betsy wanted to be a writer!) I laughed at *Mrs. Piggle-Wiggle*, I wept over *King of the Wind* and all the Lassies and Black Beauties of true hearts and fickle masters, and, having failed to make a confidante of the steel-faced librarian, when I exhausted the emotions wrought by the children's section, I became addicted to Nancy Drew.

How can I describe the pleasure of an Easter Monday or
any Saturday made special by a holiday dollar, when I squatted
before a book rack in Goldblatt's to choose a new title? There
are the smells—not ink and new paper, but jelly beans, candy
corn, and floor wax, the starched gray twill of men's work
clothes stacked on counters, the leather of pocketbooks stuffed
with tissue where the wallets and tobacco-shagged lipsticks
belong. The sounds—under-counter doors rattling across their
aluminum tracks, the dead chord of cash register keys struck
three together, the high-pitched bell of the elevator. But mostly
there am I, sitting in the burnished gold-gray light on the floor
of an alcove already sealed off as an entrance to a department
store that has since been vacant for years, reading of Nancy's
roadster and silk frocks, already doomed to nostalgia in a
world committed to nylon and—though it doesn't know it
yet—Toyotas.

I rode the bus home reading. By bedtime I would be finished,
and on the next school day I would bring my treasure to trade
with my new friend Gulsum, another addict, a Turkish girl
born in China who escaped the Reds with her father and grew
up in Australia, where she kept a pet kangaroo. Her mother
died in China, whether in childbirth or the political upheaval
I either do not recall or never knew. Her stepmother was in
the process of suing Lana Turner, whose daughter, Cheryl, had
stabbed Lana's lover to death; the lover was Gulsum's stepmother's ex-husband and the father of Gulsum's stepbrother,
John. This last she never mentioned; I knew because *The
Hammond Times* reported it, and in a school more accustomed
to petty thieves than foreign students or Hollywood connections, I remember a whisper of scandal.

What I don't remember is thinking her exotic, though I
suppose some hideous little drawer in the rigid cabinet of a
mind trained to think in linking verbs, in the unconditional
grammar of nominatives where nothing ever happens, filed

these facts. She lived in a tract house much like mine, ate her dinner at a similar formica and chrome dinette, endured the same dopey boys spitting mashed potatoes in the Woodrow Wilson Junior High cafeteria ("Look, I'm a pimple"), and marked the endless sentence of our humdrum girlhoods by a living room clock that is preserved in a picture in my album, where it summons all the hopeless innocence of an era when people realized dreams by saving S & H Green Stamps. No, she was not exotic to me, despite my impeccably eventless life; I think she was no more exotic to herself. How else to explain the avidity with which she took my latest Nancy?

Ah, Nancy Drew, now there was a world apart. We had "I Love Lucy" and English (*is, was, has been, will be*, with the boys in the back row throwing spitballs); Nancy had adventures. She was forever being knocked over the head to come to in a room stocked with black widow spiders or a house about to fall into the sea; she was less a real girl than a series of crises and rescues. But there was something else, beyond her freedom, beyond all the secrets and clues, the hidden staircases, mysterious letters, and missing maps, that distinguished Nancy's world from ours. Hers was a world of absolutes, good and evil, with no moral murk between. Was Miss Dredge, the pink-haired old lady with one gray suit who ignored the spitballs and droned on (*feels, appears, seems to be*), good? Surely she was not evil, though we all hated her and called her Miss Drudge. Was my mother good? Was I? Was Cheryl, daughter of Lana, evil? What about my father, who suffered insomnia when he worked the night shift and came out of his bedroom raging whenever I made too much noise? "Your father is a good man," my mother would explain. "He's a good provider. Now look what you've done," she would say, and I would tell the neighbor at the door that she wasn't home while she crouched behind the armchair fingering her bruise. We lived a far cry

from pretty Nancy, the good, golden-haired sleuth tracking an
underworld of dark jewel thieves, counterfeiters, and forgers,
a world in which the only passion was greed and good always
won over evil. Even then we—Gulsum and I—knew that these
mysteries we adored were useless as guides. What drew us to
them was the fact that they were lies.

5.

WHAT A REVELATION COLLEGE was to me, the discovery of
a literature that dealt in truth—in the mysteries and measures
of character, in the paradox of good and evil, not in a moral
world but a moral vision—at the same time that I fancied I
had discovered a life that was not a lie. I went home as rarely
as respectable, wore jeans before they were fashionable, affected
a lenseless pair of granny glasses, espoused unpopular causes
with no real understanding of the issues, took odd courses,
hung out at foreign films, read Ferlinghetti, and somehow
figured all this made me an honest—i.e., moral—person. But
I also read Chaucer, Shakespeare, Milton, Keats, Wordsworth,
Byron, Blake, Joyce, Woolf, Hawthorne, Hemingway, Faulkner,
Fitzgerald, et al., for I majored in English, doubling up hours
and taking correspondence courses to make up the fifteen
credits beyond the forty-five maximum in any one subject that
would count toward a diploma. My minor was more literature,
comparative, and to this day I embarrass myself in French
pronunciation, having been so busy reading that I taught
myself the requisite languages from textbooks rather than
taking the time to slow down and learn them from the *crois-
sant*, *Wurst*, and oral drill up in 101 classes. In those days I was
into *ideas*.

I might have majored in philosophy if my freshman teacher
hadn't had such a terrible case of dandruff or made such a
clumsy near-pass. "You seem like such an interesting person,"

he said, explaining why he had summoned me to his office on the pretext of discussing my test, about which he had nothing to say. "Me?" I squeaked. When one is seventeen, decisions are made out of such silliness: He was no more interested in my mind than I was in his body, and I was shocked, because I admired his mind, but in my awareness of the white scurf on his sweater (he sat much too close), I understood that the body was precisely what I missed in his class, where we made sense of life without the pleasure of experiencing it first through the senses. I chose English, and in that choice nearly all the turns my life has taken since, because what I read in those classes was at once intellectual and visceral.

That is what I say about the choice now. At the time I had no such word in my vocabulary. I made it on instinct, the same that led me to decide in second grade my ambition to be a writer. I liked stories; I liked poems; I liked the illusion they gave me of learning things firsthand. *Learning* would have been a key word then, for I was serious and did not know I could seriously admit that I chose literature for the pleasure of it.

One discovers—and deepens—that pleasure by stages. If the readers who make best-sellers never leave the first and second stages, in which one reads for entertainment or the satisfaction of an emotional need, serious students know the third: the thrill of honing in on the meaning, the triumph of discovering that all great literature has a theme and that the theme nearly always has to do with morality or, in its narrower sense, ethics. Perhaps even then I knew there was a fourth, an appreciation for style, that grace of the acute word and accurate rhythm. The appreciation for what writers call texture, that *sine qua non* of sensory detail, often comes later, for, although the tools are available to any six-year-old, it seems to take some knowledge of the craft to raise the appreciation to the level of conscious and legitimate delight. This fifth is not the last stage—there is another, in which all the pleasures unite and the work becomes whole for the reader—but the love for texture and the love for the language are the ones that seduce the writer.

6.

ART, I SOMETIMES TELL my writing students, is a perfect and constantly changing balance of cruelty and nostalgia.

I am quick to explain to them that by *nostalgia* I do not mean *sentimentality*, though likely I do. I am attached to the things of this world, which I suspect I measure more by my attachment than by their own worth, the eternal week of the weeping cherries, the starburst of time in an S & H clock. It is sentiment that makes phenomena of them, just as it is sentiment that lingers over the telling quirks of character, the cactuses on Emma Bovary's windowsill, Dolores Haze's hand stretched out to take Humbert Humbert's figurative penny, long after the intellect has summed up the person. It is, to my mind, something akin to what Gertrude Stein means by the noun in that odd essay on poetry and grammar. Prose, she says, loves the verb; poetry loves naming. For me, the greatest pleasure of literature comes half from that poetry of naming, from the word that evokes not only the substance but also the emotions the writer would have us attach to it, a poetry that is as much a part of the best prose as of any lyric. Literature serves the desire to possess the world by giving it a name.

It balances on our sense of loss.

For as much as nostalgia comes from loss—our impending sense of death, informed by all the little things we lose along the way—so does the cruelty that is our cold knowledge of it. One might call it irony, but it is also discipline.

Having named the thing, we subject it to the truth of action. The way in which it yields is all the pleasure.

7.

THE WRITER IS THE VOICE of humankind, speaking to the race of the individual and to the individual of the race, witness to the imagination, the intellect, history, and life of his or her time. Literature is the record. By it I enlarge the bounds of my sympathy, for as it calls me to imagine that I am part of some other, I join company in a way that I cannot in any other social endeavor. I am permitted to know characters in mind, dream, and body, in a way that I will never know even those people who are so close to me as my husband and son.

Tonight I will read.

Tomorrow I will return to writing my novel.

These are not lonely acts.

By them, in their heightened moral climate, I cast myself outside the dumb glory of nature and come to know Eve. I have tasted the fruit. In truth I have found it most delicious. I reach for the word and invent my own garden.

THE END OF COUNTERCULTURE

———

PERHAPS BECAUSE I MAKE photographs, my recollection of time and place is almost always a memory of light. For me, the words *Richmond, Virginia* evoke the pearl gray August twilight in which I first saw the buildings of the Fan. Parisian light, I call it, though the air was sweet with tobacco, a luster webbed with lilac shadows and gossamer with dew. To an inexperienced would-be writer/photographer accustomed to the straightforward sunshine and foursquare architecture of the Midwest, the silky dusk deepening over the brick bays and crenellated towers, the cast iron verandas and cobblestone alleys seemed to promise a life every bit as romantic, as bohemian and free as the legendary Left Bank.

The year was 1970. It was a bad year for the counterculture: the year before, Students for a Democratic Society had
imploded; Weatherman, its renegade army and vanguard
symbol, vanished underground only to blow itself up in a
bizarre accident in a Greenwich Village townhouse; President
Nixon asked Congress to set stiff penalties, including death, for
the illegal use or transportation of explosives, legislation that
seemed directed less toward genuine acts of terrorism than at
the rebellious young left in general. That fall, for the first time
since 1965, a Harris poll would find the number of students
who considered themselves radical or far left in decline. In
May, Nixon had invaded Cambodia despite overwhelming
opposition to the Vietnam War; among the hundreds of
ensuing protests was Kent State, where the Ohio National
Guard fired into a crowd of demonstrators, killing three white
students and a teenaged runaway. In New York, police looked
on as hard hats beat protestors with lead pipes; in Mississippi,
at Jackson State College, police fired into a women's dormitory,
killing two black students; and in Georgia, police killed six
African Americans *accused* of rioting. Within weeks of my first
night in Richmond, Jimi Hendrix and Janis Joplin would both
overdose and die. Such an accumulation of setbacks seems
more portentous in retrospect. 1968 hadn't seemed such a good
year either—the assassinations of Martin Luther King Jr. and
Bobby Kennedy, the mass arrests following the student take-
over at Columbia, the establishment of a domestic war room
at the Pentagon, the Miami riots, the disastrous Democratic
National Convention in Chicago and subsequent election
of Richard Nixon, whose "bad cop" sidekick Spiro Agnew
dismissed the entire peace movement as "an effete corps of
impudent snobs"—but in 1968, the whole world watched as
the counterculture flowered.

For me, 1970 promised the camaraderie and purpose the '60s
had failed to deliver—that is, seemed to deliver to everyone

else but passed over me. After four dreary years of graduate school (his) and make-do employment (mine), Virginia
Commonwealth University had offered my then-husband a
job. The South was to be the scene of my liberation, and any
preconceptions I brought with me (more moonshine and
rednecks than moonlight and magnolias) were annulled by
that first stroll down Franklin Street, across Monroe Park and
through the fragrant, softly lit brick and brownstone campus.
The South—Richmond—looked, as we used to say, far out.

I was twenty-five years old. In 1966, when I graduated from
Indiana University, the counterculture so soon to be a divisive
household word was not yet a mass market concept. SDS had
just begun to infiltrate campus consciousness through a series
of Friday forums in Dunn Meadow, the former sheep pasture
that provided the university with its largest open space, but the
status quo seemed unlikely to flinch in the face of two-dozen
students in khakis, oxford shirts, and shirtwaist dresses argu-
ing that U.S. involvement in the Vietnam War was wrong. I
doubt scarcely more than another dozen students knew there
was a war in Vietnam. Who could have predicted that within
two years Dunn Meadow would be seething with antiwar
slogans and acid rock beneath a pungent haze of massive
misdemeanor?

Certainly not I, though as an undergraduate writing and
photography student, I had attached myself to a vaguely arty
circle—meaning that I wore jeans instead of pleated skirts,
preferred foreign films to Doris Day, and listened to Bob
Dylan. In my senior year I covered the art beat for an underground paper. Hardly radical. Politically I was unconscious,
though I had participated in a civil rights demonstration two
years before and had a boyfriend who went to Selma. Like
a lot of lazy liberals I let moral instinct pass for politics. On
a campus as large as Indiana's such eccentricities blended
in. But when I married a graduate student that fall of '66, I

committed myself less to an anticipation of the future (which is easy to promise away) than to a grinding, daily present, an indefinite stay in a college town that I knew only through the college.

I might have moved a thousand miles away, so profound was my culture shock. Small, conservative, poor, settled upward from Appalachia rather than downward from the urban North, Bloomington offered little sympathy to an unskilled, vaguely bohemian liberal arts grad, only a series of dead-end jobs that would effectively sequester me from my generation. I went to work in the darkroom of a TV tuner factory, where I was required to sign a loyalty oath that was such a jumble of pledges to my company and my country I wouldn't understand the perverse sense it made until the '80s, when the country went back to school in Reaganomics. The oaths were used to weed out workers suspected of sympathy toward the unions that periodically tried to organize the electronics plants in labor-cheap southern Indiana. I made fifty dollars a week, before taxes. When I quit to work in the darkroom of a newspaper that offered me ninety (a violation of my oath), the plant's personnel manager called the paper to complain that it was a mistake to pay a woman that much money. As it turned out, he was right, for the male photographers refused to let me touch their film, and I soon got fired because I had nothing to do.

The worst year was the one I spent entombed as a clerical worker in the IU Business Building, where even coffee breaks were supervised and I was forbidden to respond to the graduate assistant who had seen me with my husband at the Von Lee, the art film theater that had yet to degenerate to a porn house, and tried to strike up a conversation. My job was to paste mailing labels on a magazine called *Business Horizons*. After that I spent three years as a copy editor for the IU

Research Center for the Language Sciences, where I employed my education to argue pronoun reference and subject/verb agreement with a series of Hungarian, Finnish, Estonian and Turkish linguists who considered their command of the English language to be beyond reproach. It was a much more lively job than those I'd held before, but no matter where I worked I had to be there eight to five, and in those days even darkrooms had a dress code. I spent the psychedelic years in A-line dresses and stacked heels, in bed by midnight in order to be up before seven, and no matter how many lunch hours I lingered in Dunn Meadow, where the twenty or so button-down Students for a Democratic Society had gone home to change their clothes and come back with a thousand like minds in ragged bell-bottoms, Mexican wedding shirts, and dashikis, no matter how many blues concerts or protests or "Free University" seminars I attended, I never felt that I belonged: everyone knows real radicals don't wear pantyhose. If my boss, a Hungarian aristocrat who had fought the Russians in the 1956 revolution, made me feel like a communist sympathizer, the day-glo youth of Dunn Meadow made me look like Donna Reed.

When I got home from work, I prepared dinner, which my husband (who had turned out to be such an indifferent student it was hard to imagine he might ever complete his PhD) liked to eat from a tray in front of the *Huntley-Brinkley Report*, giving me the sensation that I watched the spectacle of the '60s that swirled all around me on TV. During those years, *Time* made a habit of reporting the *in* place for hippies each summer. One year it was the Boston Common, the next Colorado. By coincidence I was in Boston the summer the flower children decamped for the Rockies. The next year I spent two weeks at a photography institute in Aspen, which was hip enough in a chic way, but the teeming masses, the great unwashed, tuned-in, turned-on throng of fractious youth, were gone. To be sure, I thought Abbie Hoffman and Jerry Rubin silly, believed the militant rhetoric of the new SDS leadership to be a wrong turn, and suspected the more-revolutionary-than-thou stance of the kids in Dunn Meadow, who felt upstaged by media attention to the University of Wisconsin, was just another Big Ten competition—but oh how I wanted into their club! I wanted to feel young.

That's what Richmond promised. The Fan District, that neighborhood of turn-of-the-century townhouses named for the shape of its branching streets, seemed an ideal set, a vivid mélange of gentrification, bohemia and slum, bordered by an art school that was the heart and soul of VCU. Indeed, one of my first contacts, a hirsute young man I accosted on the street to ask about apartments, gestured first to the handsome brick house where I might find his landlord and then proudly to the bedsheet hanging like a banner from a second story window across the street. "Grove Avenue Republic" it said in crude red letters. I had come to the hip block. The Republic, I gathered, was Richmond's radical collective, where action organized itself, though in the noonday sun its flag flapped listlessly and the Grove Avenue Republicans appeared to be asleep. I never did see a sign of life behind those windows, and within a few weeks the flag was taken in. The housing tip proved no more fruitful, for the students had arrived before us and the Fan was pretty well booked for the year. His elderly landlord invited me into his parlor, served me a Coke and told me his life story, but had no rooms to rent. Never mind—we wouldn't want to live there anyway, my husband's faculty hosts assured us as they regaled us with the crime report and drove us to the interchangeable new apartment complexes in the suburban West End. I had grown up in the suburbs; the most clearly defined agenda I had was never to live in their banal domain again. By the end of that initial contract-signing, house-hunting trip I was so dispirited by harvest gold appliances and avocado carpets that we postponed the search, arranged to put our motley furniture in storage, and took a room on the Jefferson Davis Highway in the ragged hem of the city's South Side.

The room was in one of those small, square '40s bungalows so nondescript they survived unnoticed between the Kmarts and McDonald's that had already begun to line the older routes into our cities. Actually, I would have welcomed a Kmart or McDonald's: our neighbors were a gas station next door (this was in the days when gas stations sold service instead of sandwiches and sodas) and blocks of tobacco storage sheds across the street. The room itself was the size of a walk-in-closet, dark with knotty pine, crowded by its double bed, nightstand, narrow wardrobe and straight-backed chair, on which we placed our black and white TV. There was no room for the stereo, much less records, and we had to take care not to trip over the TV cord or fan when traveling from bed to the bathroom that we shared with the owner, a retired Hungarian immigrant who was obsessed with hatred for the Gypsies. There was no phone. Our new Renault had exhausted itself on the trip and was in a shop across the river awaiting parts.

Every morning I had the choice of riding across the Lee Bridge on the back of my husband's motorcycle or remaining in the room, a choice that was binding for the day, for we had no kitchen privileges and never returned until we had gotten supper. Usually I rode across the river; on those few occasions when I was just too tired to want to wander all day long, I watched soaps and listened to our landlord rave—my husband couldn't understand his accent, but I had professional experience and it didn't take me long to comprehend that he believed we were Gypsies who intended to rob his house. He began to lock us out of the bathroom. If I had expected freedom to the tune of Janis, Jimi, the Dead, or the Stones, mine was initially enacted to the rise of accusation, melodramatic pause, and tragic flatness of the soaps.

That and the gossip of the blue-haired widows who spent their days visiting in the spacious, elegantly furnished ladies' lounge on the fifth floor of Miller and Rhoads in downtown Richmond. "M'unroes," they seemed to pronounce it, as if they had mud in their mouths: I was better at decoding Uralic and Altaic accents than Southern. In the hats and white gloves they wore to ride the bus in from the West End, they seemed caricatures of a bygone era, but for all the talk of Confederate generals they claimed as kin, the glory of the old days and "tore-to-pieces" nowadays, they acted less annoyed by the generation gap than my mother, and despite my appearance were exceedingly gracious to me. (No more pantyhose for me; I was in search of the counterculture, and in my long, long straight hair, my leather miniskirt, head-scarves and big hoop earrings I looked, well, come to think of it, like a Gypsy. It didn't occur to me that I might also look just like their grand-daughters.) They taught me one of the first lessons I learned about the South: if you want to loiter, pick a genteel place; no one then would ever be so rude as to question your right to be there. I had taken to loitering because I was homeless, unless I counted the room on the Jefferson Davis Highway where I couldn't use the bathroom or get anything to eat. I had hay fever and craved the air-conditioning of the ladies' lounge or, when I wanted the peace and quiet to read, the ornate lobby of the Jefferson Hotel, whose grand staircase had supplied the model for the one Rhett Butler ascended to the offstage rape of Scarlett O'Hara in *Gone with the Wind*.

All told, we lived on the Highway for six weeks. I found an apartment in the Fan, just a few houses up from the Grove Avenue Republic, but it came with an emphatic no-pets policy

and no place to store my bike. We had lived in no-pets buildings all those years in Bloomington; I had spent my childhood without a pet. I wanted a dog. How could I hope to join
the counterculture if I allowed my landlord to oppress me?
Reluctantly we passed and signed a lease for an apartment on
the South Side so new it was under construction.

I didn't hang out at VCU, not then, though I did later.
Charming though it was, the campus was inhospitable. If the
streets of the Fan were a wayfarer's paradise, the converted
brownstones that composed much of the university invited
only those who knew where they were going. I couldn't find
its center. The new library looked like a Sears store, and
while there was a respectable body of unkempt students and
bandana-wearing, Frisbee-catching mutts on its modest front
lawn, there was no open space, no teeming mass, no seeming
organization. We had arrived too late for me to register for
the writing and photography classes I hoped to take. Instead
I enrolled in a night school photo workshop taught by an ad
man who instructed us in fashion layouts and food photography techniques. (You beat egg whites into milk to make the
bubbles and blow cigar smoke through a rectal tube to create a
plume of coffee steam.) I don't recall what technical advice the
guest lecturer offered, only that he sang the praises of his new
double-knit slacks and prophesied a menswear revolution that
later arrived in the form of the leisure suit. I might have been
free at last, but I was as out of it as ever.

My husband was at least meeting freshmen. With his walrus
mustache and mop of curly hair, he attracted the disaffected.
One was a Vietnam vet who had turned against the war. A tall,
strikingly handsome young man who strode the campus in a
floor-length greatcoat, he claimed to have lost his rifle the day
he arrived in Vietnam, to have gone AWOL and never been
missed, to have spent his tour completely stoned. But for all

his insouciance, his account of the first demonstration that
fall (which we sat out, unaware) focused on his disgust for the
freshman girl he'd overheard enthusing to a friend, "Just think
—we've got four more years of this to look forward to!" For
him, the late-night demonstration proved more lethal than his
year in Vietnam. The police brought out their dogs, and he was
bitten on the hand. At the VA hospital where he was treated
he developed gangrene. He dropped out of school. When we
saw him next, nearly two years later, at the Democratic headquarters during George McGovern's presidential campaign, we
shook hands. All the flesh had been scraped from his palm; his
face was gaunt, his skin the jaundiced gray of tallow. I wouldn't
have recognized him.

Another of my husband's students made a project of us: he
and his roommates took us to parties in the Fan and supplied
us with marijuana. We spent a month of Sundays in their
Cherry Street apartment, watching the Redskins, drinking beer
and passing joints, but when they discovered that my husband
was twenty-eight, they failed to conceal their horror. By their
own admission they had assumed he was no more than twenty-three, more or less their age, and—this was the sticking
point—that I was still a teenager. It was as if we had betrayed
them. We couldn't seem to find our generation.

By then we had moved. (The Hungarian landlord refused
to admit the students who had come to help us load our few
possessions and stood shaking his fist at us as we backed the
U-Haul down the driveway.) Our car was out of the shop, but
I had never learned to drive, and my husband, whose parents
had given us our previous car for a wedding present on the
condition that I was never to drive it, was reluctant to teach
me. Though I had a kitchen now, if I didn't ride to campus
with my husband in the morning, I was still stranded on the
South Side for the day.

I volunteered for the Big Brother/Big Sister Program at Grace House, a community center on Floyd Avenue that served the seedier pockets of the Fan, the black strip along Main and Cary streets, and the rundown precinct just below it, Oregon Hill. The latter was a name I recognized from faculty parties, where the favorite topic of conversation was real estate. As Fan prices rose, a number of faculty turned a speculative eye south and advised us to buy on Oregon Hill. That we weren't in a position to buy anything was just as well, for, not surprisingly, the urban reclamation they predicted didn't cross Cary until long after we left Richmond. In a city where nearly everything was built of brick, a number of the houses on Oregon Hill were frame, erected in the shadow of the state penitentiary for the working class attracted by the Tredegar Iron Works in the nineteenth century, and long since fallen into such disrepair that the surviving buildings appeared marooned by those that had been torn down. That fall, as Richmond began court-ordered busing to achieve school desegregation, Oregon Hill had the highest rate of noncompliance. Monday through Friday, its streets rang with the boisterous sound of truants at play. Their accent I recognized from my years in southern Indiana: hillbillies (poor white trash is not a northern term). This was the South I had expected, and on an October Saturday, the Grace House Director of Youth Services and I began knocking on its doors to recruit Little Brothers and Sisters.

It did not seem odd to me that the Big Brothers and Sisters had already been signed up. The Grace House program followed the model of the decade's earlier community organization projects in that it recruited the helpers first, then went looking for the helpees. Having sat out the volunteer experience of the '60s I had also skipped its disenchantment. I wasn't there when Black Power disenfranchised the liberal white students who came South to register black voters. I missed the moment when the antiwar movement stole SDS's heart away from its last ERAP projects, those failed grassroots attempts to heal America community by community. I believed in community involvement. I was nearly as old as the veterans of Port Huron who dressed the moral bandwagon that the counterculture first climbed on, whose mission to create an interracial movement of the poor broke with their parents' practice of *noblesse oblige* to observe the axiom outlined by Pavel Axelrod almost a century before: "He who wishes to work for the people must abandon the university, forswear his privileged condition, his family, and turn his back even upon science and art. All connections linking him with the upper classes of society must be severed…"

They had not set out to create a counterculture but a new culture, and it was only when the difficulties of such an endeavor became insurmountable, when even the forswearing of privilege no longer admitted the white reformer into black communities (as happened, for example, in the Cleveland ERAP project that later Weatherwoman and fugitive Kathy Boudin helped organize), when they turned from the War on Poverty to the war in Vietnam, that the counterculture blossomed. In her memoir, *Growing Up Underground*, Jane Alpert speaks to the secret behind that transformation when she describes her experience as a Swarthmore student protesting conditions at an all-black ghetto school in Chester, Pennsylvania:

> I was prepared, or so I thought, for arrest, even for police brutality. But I was not prepared to find a wellspring of anger inside me, tapped by the chanting. As if hypnotized, I was frantically stamping my feet, cheering "Freedom! Now!" long after I was too hoarse to make a sound. I had stopped thinking about Franklin School, the citizens of Chester, the evils of racism and poverty. The Utopian vision that had tugged at me yesterday was gone. In its

place was something else, a fury that tore out of me with a life of its own, primitive as infancy. I was screaming against everyone and everything that had stood in my way—the boys who had rejected me, the man who had fired my father when I was nine, my absent father, my mother, my brother. I wasn't the only one in the crowd who temporarily lost control.

As protests against the war escalated, a generation of middle-class white students experienced the catharsis, the sense of personal liberation, that Jane Alpert experienced in Chester. It was a powerful drug, and by 1970, the mid '60s theoretical politics of self-sacrifice and self-denial felt as fuddy-duddy to the counterculture rank and file as the Old Lefties' socialist LID politics had seemed to the children who broke from the League for Industrial Democracy's student organization to form Students for a Democratic Society in 1962. What I failed to understand about the youth movement I so desperately wanted to join was that its first generation was already aging out and the directions I saw as diverse had been almost from the start exclusive and incompatible. By the time I went looking for my own catharsis on Oregon Hill, the students who most typified the counterculture were the least likely to volunteer, for once the youth movement caught on, it became, for all its anger about the war and outraged sense of justice, a rash but not radical, quasi-political, poorly informed, hedonistic celebration of itself that took politics as its stage. Revolution? Groovy. This was the generation that learned revolution could be fun.

It is a cliché to blame the end of the '60s activism on Kent State, but there's no denying that the massacre of middle-class children dampened the party spirit. After all, demonstrations were by then as much a part of campus life as beer blasts. When the first generation of white New Left volunteers, the Freedom Riders and civil rights workers, confronted the

institutionalized intractability and brutality of racial politics in the South, they learned what African Americans had
always known, the price for countering the prevailing culture.
Operating out of political naïveté and a largely middle-class
mentality, the counterculture's younger generation was far
more frangible. And it had already lost its cadre.

I wanted to plug in, not drop out. I recall wearing a dress to
impress our respectability upon the Oregon Hill mothers—not
that it mattered. Oregon Hill was by nature anti-institutional,
and its resistance of the Supreme Court in the form of the
school boycott hardly created a bond with higher education's
privileged "bums," as Nixon characterized peacenik students. It
was no more likely to send its children to a community center
that drew its constituency from neighborhoods both black
and white than it was to let them ride the buses to integrated
schools, no matter how I dressed. Our recruits might be among
VCU's straightest students, but by then mainstream youth
had so assimilated hippie style that it was not always apparent
at a glance who were the Marxist girls and who the Young
Republicans. Recruiting was discouraging work, without much
camaraderie, and in the end we had our greatest success along
Main and Cary streets, our least on Oregon Hill. Even so, we
assembled a volatile mix, and I remember a great deal of racial
tension at the Grace House Halloween party, at which one of
the children picked my pocket.

My own Little Sister was an eleven-year-old black girl
named Barbara whom I continued to see for the next two
years, though by Christmas the Grace House program had
all but dissolved as group activities dwindled and volunteers
lost interest and drifted away. She lived with her mother, aunt,
brother, and two sisters in a three-room apartment that reeked
of roach spray and, in the winter, kerosene. Her twelve-year-
old sister was also in the program, but soon soured on her Big

Sister and sometimes accompanied us on our twice weekly excursions. Yvonne was a much more flamboyant and street-wise child than Barbara, the baby of the family. So was their handsome fourteen-year-old brother Nat, who asked me if I had a boyfriend. "She got a husband," Barbara answered for me. "Well, girl, you have got yourself a lover," he exclaimed and doubled with laughter. Once I asked Barbara what he planned to do when he grew up, and she looked at me with disbelief. "Do?" she said. "He do what everybody do. He get drafted and be killed." She had an utterly disingenuous way of leaving me breathless. "Doesn't that upset you?" I nearly wept. "Sure it upset me," she responded. "When it happen." After a minute she added matter-of-factly, "Your husband just teach school. He white." For Christmas more than anything she wanted a PJ doll, Barbie's golden-haired little friend. She didn't have a Barbie; I don't think she'd ever owned a doll. That season Mattel was marketing its first black Barbie, a short-haired eleven-and-a-half-inch Julia attired in the crisp nurse's whites Diahann Carroll wore in the TV series of the same name, touted for breaking the primetime color barrier by portraying a professional black woman. *Black was beautiful*, and I'm sure I hoped that Barbara would solve my squeamish white liberal dilemma for me once she saw that she could have a glamorous black role model to play with. Instead she gasped, "What's that colored doll doing up there with all those white dolls?" For there on the shelf in Miller and Rhoads among the bride dolls and ballerinas, the blue-eyed baby dolls in christening lace and buxom blond Barbies with their trunks full of fur capes and gold lamé, stood Julia in a uniform that might as well have been the maid's. I sewed PJ an entire wardrobe of leisure wear and frills. Someone else would have to raise her consciousness, I decided, or perhaps I simply realized how absurd it was to think, as if it were a Christmas gift, that I could, or should, bestow black pride. My enduring memory of her family is an image of them gathered before the TV, laughing so hard that tears rolled down their cheeks as Doris Day did the funky chicken.

Initially I had also been slated to teach photography to all the children, something I was utterly unqualified to do, requiring as it would not just the technical know-how I did possess but a gift for helping children discover themselves through art. The idea was the idealistic brainchild of the Grace House Youth Services Director, who enthusiastically ordered cameras, though the group so quickly strained that the only "pupil" I recall working with was Barbara. She was a less than eager student. "What you want me to take a picture of?" she whined. "It's not what *I* want, it's what *you* want," I insisted. "I don't want to take a picture," she said. "Yvonne?" I suggested. "Who want a picture of her ugly face?" Barbara pouted. We gave up camera work. We went to the museums and the zoo; we went shopping; we baked cakes; we played Monopoly and Clue. Once I suggested a walk in Hollywood Cemetery, the overgrown gothic graveyard overlooking the Kanawha Canal and James River below Oregon Hill. "What for?" she asked. "You got somebody in there?" She was the classic antidote to the romantic zeal of the reformer, as obdurate and winsome as, well, a little sister. It didn't matter that Grace House gradually vanished from our lives. I loved her.

Still searching for the experience that would define my place in the counterculture, I joined a citizen's group called Homework that was mounting a campaign to enforce the city's housing code and shut slumlords down. With the exception of the Grace House Youth Director and another former VISTA volunteer who had elected to remain in the service of one of Richmond's social agencies, it turned out to be a group of middle-aged Lefties who did their good work and went home without any unnecessary joviality or bonding. I made a lot of phone calls. We didn't have an office, except for the month of our campaign, when we rented a storefront in one of the cast iron buildings on a block of East Main Street that, despite the efforts of Richmond's active preservationists, was soon razed to make way for one of the first of the skyscraper banks that dominate the contemporary Richmond skyline. The local news did a thirty-second feature, and though we met on through the following fall I don't recall that we accomplished anything. I might have forgotten the experience entirely, but it all came back several years ago when I read *Democracy Is in the Streets,* James Miller's history of the New Left through 1968. For the youth culture democracy might have taken to the streets, but for Homework in 1970, freedom was still "an endless meeting."

One of the Homework volunteers, who belonged to the Women's International League for Peace and Freedom, invited me to participate in a weekly vigil outside the Army/Navy Recruiting Office. I was ready for the streets, but instead of thousands, or even a dozen shouting tie-dyed youth, I joined a silent, orderly line of more forty and fifty-something Old Lefties who dressed just like my parents. (Years later I would stand in a similar line outside the Armed Forces Recruiting Office in Greensboro, North Carolina, to protest US interference in Central America, but by then I had long since ceased to be the youngster in the group.) We held a few polite signs aloft while the Richmond police took our pictures. I was aware that the photographs were being turned over to the CIA, for the American Civil Liberties Union had already filed a class action against the Richmond police on behalf of demonstrators who had been subjected to illegal surveillance. I attended the trial alone, for everyone else who was interested was a witness. The gist of the ACLU argument was that police cooperation with the federal government's illegal surveillance of its own citizens was an act of intimidation that effectively discouraged them from exercising their First Amendment rights. Upon mounting the bench, the judge announced that although he would find in favor of the police, he would hear the case if the ACLU was determined to waste taxpayers' money. Throughout the morning's testimony, he routinely harassed the witnesses, at one point chiding a young law student who had turned away from a demonstration out of fear for his career that if he was that big a sissy he might as well not get out of bed. The ACLU lost, and my picture went into the government files on subversive activity, even though I couldn't seem to find any.

We moved to the Fan and fell in with its circle of younger faculty. Most were from the Art School, which so dominates the District that even in the New Left's heyday Richmond was more bohemian than radical, its slant on culture less political than aesthetic, something I understood only later. Only once in the two years I lived there did my attempts at political commitment and our social life merge, that first April when I rode to Washington with two of our friends to attend what turned out to be the nation's last big antiwar demonstration. Failing to find a Virginia contingent, we lined up with Women's Lib, but there was a male in our party (not my husband, who had stayed home to grade papers), and one of the marshals kicked him out. Afraid of losing one another, we dropped back and marched up Pennsylvania Avenue with his colleagues, the Librarians for Peace. A hippie with a megaphone stood atop a VW bus reading off the banners as the marchers reached the Mall. "Welcome, Chicago Business Executives for Peace," he shouted. "We look forward to your contribution." Behind us a group chanted, "We won't hide/ you can't run/the faggot you hate may be your son!" We stood in line for the portable toilets and spread our blanket on the grass to listen to the speeches, so garbled by the loudspeakers they might have been Greyhound bus arrivals and departures. It was a gorgeous spring afternoon, and beneath the lazy blue sky people were taking off their shirts and tipping their faces toward the sun. As vendors moved through the crowd hawking T-shirts and buttons, it seemed more like a fair than a protest. A few organizers tried to recruit marchers for a more militant march on May Day the next week, but the crowd was much too diverse, radical and liberal, young and old, hip and not, to unite beneath a Red banner. Though a small May Day fracas did come off, the cathartic shouting, the glory days for civil disobedience, and salad days of the symbolic arrest were over. The Movement had passed its zenith.

But Richmond's counterculture had a last hurrah. We had delayed our move to the Fan because I wanted a dog, which a student of my husband's supplied that first October. She was a pouting ten-week-old puppy who was as adorable and ridiculous in appearance as her lineage might suggest: half border collie, one quarter basset hound, one quarter cocker spaniel. From her basset/spaniel sire she inherited her short legs, long ears, mournful face, and plaintive wail; from her border collie mother a long, silky tricolor coat, keen intelligence, and complicated psyche. We named her Lemon on the theory that everything else we had owned turned out to be one, and during the year that I studied writing and photography at VCU, she became a fixture on the campus. Whenever I went to class or the library to meet friends, I tied her outside the Rotunda, which served as a student commons before the block where Barbara lived was razed to make room for a student union. On October 26, 1971, while I was listening to Kate Millett speak at the Mosque, a student with a hot dog held too loosely in his hand passed within the length of Lemon's leash. She grabbed the wiener; he went inside to call the dogcatcher. By the time I arrived the officer had rounded up all the loose dogs on

campus and students were pouring from the buildings to fill
Shafer Court, students in fringed leather vests, tie-dyed shirts,
headbands, army jackets, beads, boots, sandals, and American
flags. The antiwar movement was winding down, and
Watergate, with its ho-hum legacy of cynicism, the corruption
that fails to outrage because it is assumed, had yet to happen;
the country was about to hit a recession that would make
cleaning up one's act to get a job upon graduation seem more
urgent, but here was an issue that youth could still rally against:
authority in the form of the most unpopular man in town,
the dogcatcher. Someone let the air out of his tires. Someone
else opened the back of the truck, and the impounded animals
leapt to freedom. Hurling threats and insults, the crowd began
to rock the vehicle. Through the windshield the man's face
looked ashen. By the time a convoy of squad cars arrived, the
mob had spilled into Franklin Street and was blocking traffic. There was a stand-off of an hour, but just as the antiwar
movement had peaked in the month following the invasion of
Cambodia, so had the military approach to law and order at
Kent State. In the end the mob dispersed without tear gas or
mace, and the police escorted the dogcatcher's limping vehicle
off campus. In the alley behind Franklin Street, where one of
my husband's students had hidden her, I liberated Lemon. She
wagged her tail and licked my face.

"Bad dog," I scolded. I went home, filled out my application
to grad school, and when I finished got a job.

When I remember leaving Richmond, I see that time
and place in another light: this a cold October rain that has
replaced the fragrance of warm brick, tobacco and vanilla that
lingers in the Fan each fall with the sour smell of decay and
coming winter. I am walking Barbara home from the Grace
House Halloween party held on the VCU campus at Rhoads
hall. She doesn't mind, but *I* do: one of the other children has

called her a nigger. Or perhaps she minds but what she minds is not something she would tell a white sister. Or maybe what she doesn't tell me is everything she wouldn't have to tell a black one. Another child has stripped my wallet. A heel has come off my boot: I am hobbling, my hair sticks to my face and spikes of Halloween mascara streak my skin. At the party I have discovered what I have tried not to know for days, that the man who has been my lover has deserted me for a new, and younger, girl. When we reach the veranda in front of Barbara's house, she stands on the top step and squints down. "You look old when you get wet," she says, and in that cold, flat, gray light I am face to face with the realization that I do not love my husband and my lover does not love me, that I am a dabbler and a dilettante who doesn't know how to see or what she has to say, that I am looking for the multitude because I have not found myself, and I have no idea what I am going to do with the rest of my life or how to get it started. "I am old," I said, though I know now that I was young.

Or this light too: the orgiastic, many-colored strobes that make a herky-jerky of the final movements of the touring cast of *Hair*, which has come so late to Richmond that I am almost embarrassed to sit watching in the darkened Mosque. When the play is over and the yellow houselights have come up, the audience takes to the stage. Accountants in muttonchops, bell-bottom suits and freeway-width pink and yellow Peter Max ties are dancing enthusiastically with their wives. Walking up the aisle I think *counter* doesn't fit. It's the culture now.

GEOGRAPHY FOR WRITERS

———

"When I was seven I said to my mother, may I close my door? And she said, yes, but why do you want to close your door? And I said because I want to think. And when I was eleven, I said to my mother, may I lock my door? And she said yes, but why do you want to lock your door? And I said because I want to write."

—DOROTHY WEST

I.

"AN AUTHOR IN HIS BOOK must be like God in the universe, present everywhere and visible nowhere," Gustave Flaubert decreed. But if for the reader the writer is at most a disembodied voice and the book a finished product, a world made whole, for the writer the writing, whatever else it is or becomes, is always also a physical act and the rooms in which the act took place as much a part of the book as whatever places the work itself evokes. At writers' conferences would-be writers often ask the celebrities where, when, and how they write, as if the answers might be secrets that will transform them into published authors, but there is another fascination with the

rooms where writers write that is born of the essential contradiction of those spaces. These are the rooms writers enter in order
to exit, the place where the writer both is and is not, the locus
where the body sits—or stands or lies—while the mind explores
other territory, an outer landscape that may bear no resemblance
to the inner landscape of the writer's creation, though E.L.
Doctorow recalls once typing a sentence about the house in
which he sat, stymied by the blank page, that turned into the first
sentence of *Ragtime,* and anyone desiring a tour of the rented
houses where Vladimir Nabokov wrote during his two decades
in America need look no farther than the pages of *Lolita, Pale
Fire,* and *Pnin.* Richard Yates created the claustrophobic images
of the suburbs that appear in *Revolutionary Road* sitting in a well
house that measured five by eight feet.

The first place I remember inventing a story was not behind
a closed door but in public, in a cinder block classroom with a
bright green chalkboard in a school so new that a year or two
before it and nearly all the land around it had been prairie. The
tract neighborhoods had yet to settle into the landscape, and
the small houses and cement stoops seemed to jut grotesquely
from the muddy plain of their unseeded lawns. Unlike Dorothy
West I took no time to think, but simply raised my hand and
stood, never doubting that another sentence would follow from
the first. Stories came easy in second grade show-and-tell, for
the longer and more labyrinthine they became, the less time we
had left for arithmetic. I've forgotten those tales now, of course,
forgotten whatever kingdoms or forests they traveled, but I
remember the blond kid-sized desks and pale green grid of the
cinder block walls as distinctly as if they were the covers of a
book.

It was in the junior high wing of the same school that I first
recall writing a story, in a stenographer's notebook I carried
from class to class, waiting for study hall to pen the next chapter.

"She's writing a *novel*," my boyfriend boasted to anyone who
would listen. I wanted to write a novel because I liked reading
them, though my sense of what a novel did was formulaic. I
had grown up on the Bobbsey Twins (my mother's choice) and
Nancy Drew, but if the Bobbseys were insipid, the freedom of
the girl detective was inspiring—she was always behind the
wheel of her blue roadster, on her way to a ranch, a farm, or
charming old inn where things disappeared and went bump in
the night. There were treasure maps, ghosts, missing fortunes,
long-lost cousins; unlike the flat, featureless streets and fluo-
rescent classrooms that made up my corner of Hammond,
Indiana, her world was full of moss-covered mansions, hidden
staircases, leaning chimneys, secret caves. Girls' boarding
school novels were another favorite, and the Dana Girls, also
a Stratemeyer series, offered both dormitory pranks and the
dangers of a whodunit. Not surprisingly, my own novel was
a mystery with sister sleuths, though evidently I had less of a
nose for clues than my childhood heroines, for I abandoned it
long before the mystery resolved. It was the ambience of those
books that drew me—even then I knew the plots were routine,
the syndicated characters one-dimensional and unrealistic—
what interested me were the places, the weather, the props,
everything that made up what I thought of as a book's geography. What attracted me most to reading and writing was the
atmosphere that books created.

In college, I graduated from a steno book to a typewriter, a
used Remington manual housed in heavy gray steel, a machine
so sturdy that it is probably still working if its owner can
find ribbons. The first thing my instructor said to me when I
enrolled in a creative writing class was that he hoped my birthday came soon and that someone would give me a new ribbon.
I hated changing them. Invariably I fumbled the metal spools,
spilling big loops of red and black nylon and taking up the
slack with fingers so smudged they wouldn't come clean even

in the shower, and so I used them until the keys wore holes in the fabric and the words grew so faint on the page my instructor might have done better to read them with his fingertips like Braille, though my memory of the little red shadows inked beneath the dim gray letters is indelible. I made a backing sheet with a heavy black line drawn in Magic Marker at the bottom margin to keep from running off the page, rolling it through the carriage until it was as puckered and limp as old seersucker. These days I forget how to insert an accent or a running head from one computer to the next, but the texture of those backing sheets remains as familiar to my fingers as my own skin.

From the moment I got the typewriter I composed at the keyboard. Paragraphs looked so much more like themselves typed out in pica than spelled out in cursive's loose sprawl. Dialogue written by hand didn't speak; characters had no breath; doors wouldn't open; action refused to rise. I sat on the bed in my dorm room to type. It was a room with dormers, casement windows, and attic slopes on the third floor of a gothic stone hall in a wooded quad on the rolling green campus of Indiana University, as romantic a setting as any fictional boarding school bedroom, fit for the creation of something of genius, though I couldn't fool myself that anything I wrote there came even as close as not bad—or maybe I could have fooled myself if I'd only managed to fool my classmates and instructor.

My writing classes were held in Ballantine Hall, and I hung out with my classmates in the lounge that was on the first or second floor, a windowless room lined with machines that dispensed bitter coffee into thin paper cups. The air was thick with our smoke, so ropey and gray you couldn't tell the color of the walls. It was the kind of room that made you feel like a writer, more than any room where writing is actually done, and needless to say we talked a lot of shit.

I was accepted into Indiana's MA Program in Creative
Writing but married instead—I say *instead* because I had a
student husband to support, and I spent the first year of my
marriage entombed in a windowless office in the Indiana
University School of Business, too exhausted by hopelessness
and frustration to write. Although university policy allowed
staff to take a class each semester and make up the time, my
boss understood the policy to mean that I was permitted to
take shorthand, not creative writing. She seemed to take so
much pleasure in denying my request that years later, in the
single act of revenge I ever committed by writing, I would
put that deadly office and malevolent office manager into my
otherwise unautobiographical first novel.

When my husband passed his PhD exams and we moved
to Richmond, Virginia, I enrolled in an undergraduate fiction
workshop that met in the chapel of a former convent that
housed the English Department at Virginia Commonwealth
University. Across the river, upstairs, in the second bedroom of
our modern townhouse apartment, I wrote at an old wooden
kitchen table salvaged from my parents' basement. It was
painted white and had a deep crack, though it would last
several more years and I would write on it again, in another
apartment in another city, before the crack widened and the
table split in half. When we moved to the Fan, I returned it to
the kitchen and set up an office in the spare room that overlooked a gangway so narrow sunlight never fell across the floor,
but even though I was beginning to publish I had gone as far
as I could on my own, and so the next fall I packed up a green
card table that had been taking up space a closet and moved
to the mountains, where I enrolled in the MA Program at
Hollins College.

There I lived on a big estate southwest of Salem with a poet
from Nebraska. We shared a small cottage attached to the back

of a former hunting lodge occupied by an exiled Cuban archi-
tect, his wife, and their servant TaTa, an astonishingly small
woman from the Yucatán who spoke almost no English. The
youngest of their five children was away at boarding school
and the rest were grown; so TaTa liked to fuss over us, leaving
little treats on our pillows and serving us lunch on the patio,
always followed by a course of bleu cheese and guava jelly. No
writers' colony has pampered its residents more. Though my
bedroom/studio was only a corner of the big L-shaped living
room screened off by a bookcase, outside we had nearly three
hundred acres of woods, a stream with a waterfall, a lake, a
pond, tennis court, swimming pool, enormous pasture, and use
of the horses in the blue and white barn. I walked the trails
thinking about characters and plots. When a friend went away
for a weekend, we stayed in her third-floor apartment in an old
house on a hill in rural Cloverdale, and I wrote a short story
titled "An Interview with Rosie Tomato" at her desk, gazing
out her window at the mountains but seeing the streets of
Richmond instead. I would write about Richmond for years
after I left, the cobblestone alleys scented with the tobacco
curing in the sheds south of town somehow more vivid than if
I were at my desk back in the Fan. Perhaps I already knew that
I would never really live in Richmond again.

That Christmas I traded my Remington manual for a new
electric portable, and in the spring, while my husband visited
for the week of his break, I took my card table outside and
ran an extension cord, not to disturb him while he napped. I
was working on a story called "Disasters," and aptly enough
the pages blew into the lake. The following summer, the last
I would spend with my husband in Richmond, I revised the
stories for my collection sitting on the bed in our air-condi-
tioned bedroom while the Watergate hearings played out on
the TV beneath the stained glass panel in the center of the bay

window. I sent the manuscript to LSU Press just before I left
for the MFA Program at Arkansas. I hadn't intended to go,
hadn't even applied, but when the university made an offer, I
fled the marriage and enrolled. In Fayetteville I drafted what
would become the title story of my collection over a weekend
that my new boyfriend and I spent dog-sitting for a friend in
a furnished A-frame out at Beaver Lake. There was a mattress
in the loft where we slept, but no chairs, and I wrote "Helping
Muriel Make It Through the Night" standing at a ping-pong
table while my boyfriend glared at me from the cot that served
as a sofa because he wanted to go swimming. Though he was
a poet, like my estranged husband, also a poet, he resented
the time that *I* spent writing, the time spent without him in
that room inside my head. "You're like a dog with a bone," my
first husband used to complain, and though nothing official
had been decided between us, when I called him in January to
report that LSU Press had accepted my book, he asked for a
divorce.

That summer I moved with the man who would become my
second husband to a small furnished house at the foot of a hill
behind the university physical plant, where I would begin my
first novel. Michael wrote in the spare bedroom where his son
stayed on overnight visits; so I set up shop in our bedroom,
at an old art-deco vanity that had a center well flanked by
two pedestals of drawers. As a desk, it wasn't much, though
I remember it with the special fondness one reserves for the
chipped plate, the broken handle, the book whose binding still
bears the tooth marks of the long departed dog. My typewriter
migrated each time I hit the carriage return, and every few
lines I had to reposition it to keep the carriage from banging
against the drawers. All that fall I wrote at night while Michael
was out covering games on his beat as a sportswriter for the
Springdale News. Somewhere I had acquired a rusty gooseneck

lamp, which cast a ring of yellow light across the page, the only light in the dark house. I felt as if I were wrapped in a cloak of black velvet, writing inside a cozy hood lined in bright satin. It was so quiet I might have been underwater, with no need to breathe, suspended as I was in that golden pool of light. When Michael returned after midnight, I would start at the crunch of his tires in the driveway, rising from the vanity bench like a blind fish emerging from a cave, a dreamer surfacing from a shimmer of sleep. Then I would walk through the house switching on lights and fetch two beers and we would sit up the rest of the night listening to music and talking.

That was my apprenticeship. I remember it by the rooms that I wrote in—by the cracked white kitchen table that never appears in the story "Consumption" but is nevertheless where the unnamed husband drowned in his waterbed; by the tiled White Tower in downtown Richmond, where I sat scribbling notes for "Post Cards" while the janitor swept all around me, the idea for the story having popped into my head as I stood staring at the picture-menu on the light strip above the counter; by the ping-pong table where Muriel Moore changed her last name to Cigar, by a hoop of light on the ridiculous vanity where Janie Hurdle came out of the basement to learn how to play her clarinet.

2.

IT WAS BECAUSE WOMEN had not generally had spaces of their own or independent incomes that Virginia Woolf insisted a woman must have money and a room of her own if she is to write fiction. Money, of course, means independence from the husbands or boyfriends who resent the time she spends outside their universe. But the room of her own is as symbolic as it is physical, for the physical room is only the outward shape of an interior space. Though it was—and still is—a struggle to find the interior space, for me it was not a struggle to find the physical space, because any space would have done. The only requirement for a writer's room, according to my colleague Craig Nova, is that the writer be bored by it, which is to say that it is not the room that should claim the writer's attention. I suspect I remember the places where I wrote so intensely not just because I spent so much time in them but because they are the outward shape that recalls the inner one. Whether I wrote well there matters less than the fact that I wrote, and through those rooms I reconnect to that process in a way that I do not through the work alone. They are the way I reclaim my stories, what makes all the words since given over to the public still mine.

To imagine other writers in their spaces is to feel a kinship not just to their work but to them as writing fellows. In their books they play gods, but in their rooms they are humanized; in their rooms they too shake their heads, move paragraphs, list synonyms, cross out lines, and deliberate over names. When I think of writers struggling to create a space for themselves, I think first of John Cheever, perhaps because of the Walker Evans photograph of the squalid room on Hudson Street where Cheever lived and wrote when he arrived in New York, for it's that photograph I see, with its iron bedstead, sagging curtain, and water-damaged walls, though the room I think about was actually on the Upper East Side, a windowless basement cubicle beneath the apartment building where Cheever worked during the early days of his marriage. Each day he donned his only suit and a felt hat to ride the elevator with the other suits heading off to their offices; when he reached the lobby, he descended a flight of stairs to the basement, hung up the suit, and wrote in his underwear. Many of his stories were written in boxers, he later confided.

William Maxwell, who was once Cheever's editor at *The New Yorker*, liked to write in his pajamas; he turned down the office

the magazine offered him when he retired because he would
have had to put his trousers on and take the subway downtown. "What it means to me," he said, "is probably symbolic.
You can have me after I've got my trousers on but not before."
The delightful coincidence of these two writers composing
prose so graceful, so quietly elegant and beautifully clothed, in
states of undress always makes me think of the "match theme"
Vladimir Nabokov describes in *Speak, Memory*, where he
recalls the match trick performed for him by his father's friend
General Kuropatkin in 1904, on the day the General was
ordered to assume supreme command of the Russian Army
in the Far East. Fifteen years and a revolution later, long after
the magic matches "had been trifled with and mislaid, and his
armies had also vanished, and everything had fallen through,"
old Kuropatkin, in disguise to avoid Soviet imprisonment,
accosted Nabokov's father as a stranger on a bridge and asked
for a light. Like Nabokov, I prefer to think of such coinci-
dences not as happenstance but as design.

At the beginning of his career Raymond Carver often
wrote in his car, the only quiet place he could find when his
children were young and he was working nights to support
them. Is it any wonder that his early stories are so minimal
and claustrophobic? Other times he wrote in a library carrel or
at a kitchen table, which is where Louise Erdrich wrote "The
World's Greatest Fisherman," the germ of her first novel, *Love
Medicine*. Home for the holidays, she was trying to finish the
story by the January deadline for the Nelson Algren Award
and has spoken of her frustration at having to reach a stopping
place each day before family and friends came tromping in, just
as family tromps in and out of the kitchen in the story's pages.

On the other hand, Isaac Bashevis Singer called interruption a way of life; knowing that I reread "Gimpel the Fool"
wondering if Singer's ability to write in the midst of distraction predisposed Gimpel to accept the tricks played on him by

the villagers and his wife. According to E.B. White, his family made all the noise and fuss they wanted while he wrote, and Maxine Hong Kingston says she penned *The Woman Warrior* at a coffee table in her living room amid a swirl of people. How can a book so mythic have come from the mundane surface of a coffee table? "I can talk and write at the same time," she says, though later, when she acquired a study, she remembered how she had always wanted an office as a child, constructing one for herself in the pantry.

Jill McCorkle, another writer who wanted an office as a child, recalls transforming her father's shed into her work space, decorating it with dress-up clothing, a tea set, and fishing gear, because fishing with her father was her quiet time to think. Although she has an office in her house now, she says, "…sometimes the room of my own is the car parked in the grocery store parking lot, or wherever I can get it." Stephen King dreamed for years of having the sort of massive oak slab that would dominate a room, though when he got it he found he couldn't write. Although what blocked him was an alcoholic stupor, as he confides in *On Writing*, when he got sober he also replaced the desk with one half its size and moved it under an eave in the corner, evidently to find a space more conducive to writing than the self-conscious space of a Writer.

Who can forget the image of the idealistic and brash young F. Scott Fitzgerald working on "The Romantic Egoist," later published as *This Side of Paradise*, in a corner of the Officer's Club while he was stationed at Fort Leavenworth? When my stepson was small, my husband wrote in a Burger Chef while art students assembled the world's biggest hamburger in the parking lot outside; I once taught a student at a conference who wrote her story on the Greyhound bus enroute. Like most writers now, Robert Morgan takes his laptop with him, often writing in hotels. "My desk," Richard Ford says, "is more of

a concept than a thing. It's like the 'Belize desk' at the State
Department, an idea more than a place you actually sit at...
Like Emerson's giant, I carry my desk with me."

Anthony Trollope, author of the first novels to be serialized
in English, literally carried his desk with him, writing on a
lapboard in crowded train compartments, clubs, and tea shops;
in his autobiography he recounts an encounter with two of
his readers while working on *The Last Chronicle of Barset* at
the Anthenaeum Club. Overhearing a complaint about Mrs.
Proudie, wife of the bishop of Barchester, one of Trollope's
fondest creations, he confronted his critics and promised them
to kill the character within the week, which, despite their
embarrassed protests and to his later regret, he did.

Eudora Welty maintained that she could take notes
anywhere, but to write her books she always returned to the
desk in her bedroom, where she sits in profile before three
windows on the cover of *The Writer's Desk*, in the foreground
the rumpled linens of her unmade bed. Welty, of course, lived
in the house she had grown up in until she died. For most
writers in these days of temporary jobs, extended book tours,
residencies, and conference circuits, the desk is, of necessity,
more a concept than a thing. Yet I am hardly alone in my
attachment to the physical symbols of the territory the writer
inhabits. For writers such attachment may have to do with
the nature of the act. The language of the writer is concrete;
to commit to fiction or poetry is to commit to the tangible.
As Flannery O'Connor said, "We are made of dust, and if you
scorn getting yourself dusty then you shouldn't try to write
fiction. It's not a grand enough job for you." I used to envy
musicians because performance seems so cathartic. What is
the book's cathartic moment? The day the writer finishes the
manuscript, not knowing whether it will see print? The day the
agent or editor calls? Is it the morning I turn in the revisions

or the afternoon my copy comes in the mail, though others may have received theirs weeks ago, the letter carrier's not interested, and no one else is home? Creating a book is such a moveable feast it's no wonder we long to sit at the massive oak slab of a banquet table. A scarred vanity, a cracked kitchen table, dorm room bed, or Greyhound bus, it doesn't matter what we remember, as long as it's concrete.

Twenty-five years ago, reflecting the reading public's fascination with writers' spaces, *The New York Times Book Review* ran a feature on the rooms where Kingston, Joseph Heller, Mary Lee Settle, William Styron, Joyce Carol Oates, Mary Gordon, and Erica Jong worked; more recently the *San Francisco Chronicle* published "A Room with a Muse," describing the offices of Anne Lamott, Amy Tan, Lisa Brown, and her husband, Daniel Handler, better known as Lemony Snicket. Thus we can read Lemony Snicket with a mental picture of Handler writing at the gynecologist's table he uses for a desk (sans stirrups), though if this seems a bit naughty, we might recall that Voltaire outdid him by using a lover's naked back. Modesty prohibits me from conjuring the image of Victor Hugo, Benjamin Franklin, or Edmond Rostand at work, for they all preferred to write in the nude. As Franklin did, Diane Ackerman writes in the bath, laying a pine plank across the tub and composing amidst a swirl of bubbles. When the water temperature and body temperature converge, she says, "my mind lifts free and travels by itself."

Supposedly Edgar Allen Poe wrote with a Siamese cat perched on his shoulder, though it was Dante who had the more useful pet—he taught his cat to sit on a table and hold a lighted candle between its paws while he wrote at night. Beatrice may have been his inspiration, but it was a cat that lit the Florentine's way through the *Inferno*. I think of him scribbling his next *terzain* in that guttering light whenever I recall the small hoop of light on the vanity I used for a desk in the little rental house in Fayetteville.

Colette, Proust, Joyce, Robert Louis Stevenson, Edith Wharton, Walker Percy, and Truman Capote all liked to write in bed. Other writers have preferred to stand, Lewis Carroll and Virginia Woolf among them. Vladimir Nabokov wrote his novels on index cards standing at a lectern; Thomas Wolfe, who supposedly once skipped down the streets of Manhattan singing, "I wrote ten thousand words today," used the top of a refrigerator. Mark Twain kept a billiards table in the writing room of his magnificent house in Hartford and played a game every day before he wrote. The hand of Free Cell many writers now warm up with seems rather pedestrian in comparison, but neither does the computer have the visual cachet of the typewriters that used to sit on so many writers' desks, not to mention Kipling's pot of India ink or Herman Melville's quill pens, which were old fashioned even at the time he sat in the grandest room of his house imagining the tight quarters of a ship in pursuit of a white whale.

In *Writers' Houses* I can tour the homes of Marguerite Duras, Isak Dinesen, Jean Cocteau, Knut Hamsun, Dylan Thomas, Virginia Woolf, and William Butler Yeats, among others. All of the houses featured in the companion volume, *American Writers at Home,* are open for actual tours, though readers who prefer to travel by armchair can view the rooms of Mark Twain, Frederick Douglass, Hawthorne, and Hemingway through the lavish color photographs of Erica Lennard, who also did the photos for *Writers' Houses.* It's hard to imagine Charles Dickens as a debtor if you've seen his ornate desk in Bloomsbury. And to visit Hemingway's big, airy pale blue studio above his pool house in Key West is to forget for a moment that any space will do. His typewriter sits on a round table in the middle of the room with a panoramic view of the trophy heads on the wall, and I wonder if he looked up at them for inspiration while he sat there typing "The Short Happy Life of Francis Macomber" and "The Snows of Kilimanjaro."

In a review of English painter John Fisher's oil portraits of writers' spaces, Jay Parini refers to a number of his own far-flung pilgrimages to such sites of "significant dreaming... to wander their dark corridors and look out their windows, to observe their peculiar angle of vision on the outside world," recalling how he once sat at Faulkner's rickety desk at Rowan Oak observing "the peculiar light in August." Fisher, whose subjects include Chekov's bedroom and Joyce's Martello Tower, the setting that inspired the opening scene of *Ulysses*, explains that a "place closely associated with someone you already know, if only through his writing and reputation, has a resonance that acts strongly upon the imagination, all the more so when one is alone in the house." Even nineteenth-century readers were invited to experience that resonance through *Homes of American Authors*, published in 1853, and *Little Journeys to the Homes of American Authors*, which appeared serially in 1896.

Does "The Red Wheelbarrow" read the same if we hear the lines tapped out on William Carlos Williams electric typewriter in the upstairs study that overlooked his back-yard in Rutherford, New Jersey? I would rather imagine him at a cracked white kitchen table, scribbling "I have eaten/ the plums" on a scrap of brown paper. Do *The Jungle Books* lose heat if we know that Rudyard Kipling wrote them at a desk in Brattleboro, Vermont, while looking out the window at a snowy pasture? Two panes in the window of Nathaniel Hawthorne's study in the Old Manse are inscribed with playful messages he and his wife Sophia cut into the glass with her diamond engagement ring; this cheerful room with its pale green woodwork and homemade board-and-bracket desk is where he stood imagining Young Goodman Brown at the witches' meeting in the gloomy night forest. I wonder: did he reread that dark story years later, when his health had failed and he could no longer work, and revisit the bright room where he wrote it?

3.

MY FIRST NOVEL, LESSONS, moved around. Begun at the vanity in Fayetteville, it was finished six and a half years later at an oak kitchen table in my in-laws' garage. It did time on the cracked white kitchen table and even more on a desk I bought for eight dollars from a friend when she inherited her grandmother's secretary. The desk had a single drawer and deep shelves down one side. Later, when *Lessons* was published and I bought a real office desk, I painted my friend's desk white, topped it with a plastic pad, and used it for my son's changing table, stacking his diapers on the shelves that once held my drafts; later still he moved it to the garage and piled it with fishing line and reels. The final revisions of the novel—the ones requested by my editor at Houghton Mifflin—were done in closets and on the floors of spare rooms in the various houses of friends and family where we crashed the last weeks of summer before moving for a year to Princeton, New Jersey. There we occupied a furnished duplex whose previous tenants included George Garrett and Charles Wright. I began my second novel at a metal typing table missing one wing while outside Princeton's black squirrels chased one another up and down the trees and, back in Greensboro, Hilary Masters sat at my desk, the one that would become my son's changing table, working on his memoir, *Last Stands.*

Not long after *Lessons* came out I bought the big old house where my husband and I have now lived for more than a quarter of a century, though perhaps from habit I still move my writing around. I finished my second novel in a faculty study in the University of North Carolina Greensboro's Jackson Library. I completed the initial draft of my third in a closed-in side porch in a mansion rented out to artists by Greensboro's United Arts Council and revised it in the butler's pantry. I have written in the mansion's dining room and the former bedroom where I keep my dry mount press upstairs, as well as in the green upstairs office at home that overlooks my gardens and my ponds. Each essay has its home, each novel an itinerary.

This is how I map my life. Marguerite Duras said of Neauphle-le-Château, which she bought with the film royalties from her book *Sea of Troubles*, "I was alone in this house. I closed myself within it—I was afraid, of course. And then I liked it, and this house became the place where I wrote. My books come out of this house. From this light, from this garden." These are the rooms that have served as my Neauphle-le-Château, my moss-covered mansions, old attics, leaning chimneys, and secret caves. To write is to chart one's existence for oneself, even when the writer remains invisible to the reader, and the map that I have drawn is a treasure map of sorts, for what I am looking for, what all writers seek, is that trail of clues that were invisible until they appeared on the page, the scattered matches and vanished armies that reappear to order chaos into meaning, a map read in darkness that leads us to light.

A HOUSE IN FLORIDA

—

THE HOUSE HAS NONE of the characteristics one associ-
ates with an ancestral home, though it is what many sons
and daughters of Midwesterners who came of age during the
Depression will inherit. Michigan, Wisconsin, Illinois, Indiana
read the expired license plates nailed to the mailbox posts or
planted on stakes in the flower boxes that disguise the metal
skirting where the foundations should be, boxes that blos-
som nearly year-round with firecracker plants, hibiscus, and
ixoras, heat-lovers that could not survive in those cold, distant,
gray states. This is the strip of sunny Florida claimed by the
Midwest's retired working-class, this string of branch banks,

discount department stores, and franchise restaurants along the Gulf coast from Crystal River to Tarpon Springs. US 19, once a long, lonely stretch of road connecting Tallahassee to St. Petersburg and Tampa Bay, thrums with four lanes of traffic. It's not Naples, the trendy, once shabby-genteel Gulf town that now calls itself "the Palm Beach of the West Coast," or the Gold Coast, where geriatric New Yorkers behold the Atlantic from luxury high-rises that cast steep, granite-colored shadows across the beach each afternoon; the names of these towns that run one into another—Spring Hill, Hudson, New Port Richey—adorn no tourist brochures. Still this strip of West Central Florida is affluent beyond any measure its nouveau idle might have hoped during the decades of toil that lay between the blighted prospects of their youth and their pensions. "I never dreamed I could live like this," my father often said to me in the fifteen years that he spent in Hernando County before he died. "This place has everything I want," his next-door-neighbor echoed when I came down nearly five years after my father's death to clean out the house.

Most of the coast here is marshland, and the nearest beach, a narrow strip of trucked in sand, might as well be a hundred miles away as ten, but the occupants of High Point have a golf course and shuffleboard courts; if they want to swim they have a pool. What they're here for is not the beach but the weather, though neither the golf course nor the yards are lush. There are a few deciduous hardwoods and varieties of palm, but, like my father, most of these Midwesterners seem to shun trees. The dwellings themselves are modular houses, the sort that travel the interstates in halves, wide loads with the backs cut away, as if they might be dollhouses whose billowing plastic tarps hide a make-believe family just sitting down to dinner, a mommy and daddy giving thanks that Dick, Jane, and Sally have finally gone off to have families of their own. The walls

are as boneless and thin as dollhouse walls, and when I shower
in the narrow fiberglass stall of what was my father's bathroom
my elbows bump with a hollow sound that makes me swear I
feel the house roll, though it's securely parked on its cement pad.
To the insurance company this is a mobile home, but neither it
nor its neighbors are going anywhere. Only the homesick wives,
who miss the children and grandchildren and new great-grands
up North, who don't golf or spend their afternoons sunning, who
don't go to casino nights or take the line-dancing class and hate
the heat and bugs, only those reluctant residents call their retirement homes trailers.

Although they may lack the rootedness, the solidity and
memories of the houses grandparents used to live in, they
hardly fit the standard definition of trailer. The paneling may
be wood-grained paper and the ceilings breached by a strip of
plastic molding snapped over the joint of the house, but they
are spacious, comfortable, and well-appointed, with dishwash-
ers, disposals, and central air, laundry rooms, pantries, breakfast
bars, bay windows, and built-in buffets. There is more storage in
my father's two-bedroom, two-bath model than there is in my
big house back in North Carolina. Until he died, the plumbing
in my bathrooms was vintage 1923, with porcelain-handled
faucets that leaked rusty teardrops of cold down one side of the
basin and hot down the other. We always did go for opposites:
my house long on charm and short on convenience, his built for
comfort; no Persian rugs or antique loveseats here, but La-Z-
Boys protected from wear by terrycloth towels, wall-to-wall
carpet even in the bathrooms, and a wastebasket stationed beside
every chair.

The frills, the crocheted toilet paper cozies and macramé hang-
ings full of dusty silk flowers, belong to Donna, the companion
of his last nineteen years. I have told Donna that I consider all
the furnishings hers. Whatever may have belonged to my father

is little enough to give her, and anyway there's nothing I want, save my father's old seaman's trunk. This is not a handsome chest, like the antique pine trunk in my hallway at home, but an olive drab metal footlocker with his name, Joe Ives, stenciled in big block letters, stored in our basement when I was a girl, then in the back room of his apartment in Joliet after my parents divorced; before they married, it held everything he owned. Nothing else here will summon him for me, and though I hardly expected to find it standing in for a coffee table in this ash-blonde and peach Florida house, I did think it would be in his toolshed or closet. Instead in his closet are more clothes that I can imagine on my father, who wore the same gray twills to work every day of my childhood. Polyester sports jackets in pale blue, white, and lemon, plaid pants, white shoes. In his drawers are boxes full of clip-on bow ties and jewelry—tie clips, rings, even a pseudo gold chain. The bolo that he must have bought when he was thinking of retiring to El Paso still hangs on the knob of my son's door, a kind of X-marks-the-spot, Max's-room, warning-to-parents, off limits. Donna wants to sell the clothes. (Once she sold her cast-off evening gowns to my father, and he gave them to me for my birthday.) She wants to sell his tools and the half-empty bottle of cheap scotch on the floor of the linen closet, a bottle my father would have kept for guests, though he loathed entertaining because he rarely drank. He was neither a teetotaler nor a recovering alcoholic; he had an irritable bladder and spoke bitterly about his inability to tolerate alcohol. He would have liked to drink in social situations, which made him edgy, though his neighbors and the crowd that he and the gregarious Donna ran with, all remember him as a great, friendly, and helpful guy.

Helpful he was. He was a handyman who could fix anything, or so I believed when I was a child. Later I grew annoyed when he persisted in fixing things that weren't broken. The aesthetics of repair meant nothing to him—if he discovered that your stair rail wobbled he would nail a two-by-four to it, never mind that it was in your front hall—and he had a restless energy that wouldn't let him stop tinkering. It was less a habit learned from a lifetime of manual labor than part of his nature. He didn't like to have fun. He enjoyed swimming well into his old age, when he was young he liked to fish and loved the sea, but fun made him suspicious, and his greatest scorn was reserved for those who had too much of it. His backyard overlooked the seventh tee, but he never took up golf, which would have struck him as a frivolous pursuit. He was a hard worker who judged other people by how hard they worked and at what, physical labor, the skill of one's hands, being infinitely superior to mental tasks, which were, the way he saw it, barely a rung above welfare. Nor would the camaraderie of the golf course have appealed to him. Although he enjoyed his retirement and never regretted his move to High Point, he was to the end a loner who needed to keep himself busy.

He died just after noon on November 24, 1993, exactly one week after his eightieth birthday. It was the day before Thanksgiving, and I was already en route to Virginia Beach, where every year my husband and I spent the holiday with his father. Had Donna not been so distraught, she could have figured out how to reach me. Had I not spoken to my father on his birthday, I would have called.

When we got home on Sunday afternoon, it was my ten-year-old son who said brightly, "I wonder who called us while we were gone," and pushed the button on the answering machine.

The first message was not from Donna but from my father's next-door-neighbor, who, unlike the medical examiner of Hernando County, got right to the point. To a background of radio dispatches and sirens she said, "This is Joe Ives' neighbor. He has committed suicide and would you please call

Donna. The ambulance is here to take him away now." I do not remember my son's reaction. Though I later talked with him about what had happened, for the moment I was, as the cliché goes, frozen in place. There were other messages, interspersed with hang-ups and friends' cheery *Hi's*, one from the medical examiner asking me to call him about "an incident in Hernando County," and several from Donna, who begged me to call her more desperately each message than she had on the last. Not one of the callers thought to say what day it was or what time. The medical examiner couldn't be reached. The neighbor hadn't left her name or number, and Donna wasn't home.

My husband was still outside. There had been a storm while we were gone, and when I came out, he was raking sticks and leaves from our elderly next-door neighbor's driveway. "Hell of a place to be during a storm," my father had said the first time he came to visit—it was the second thing he said to me, though we had not seen each other for several years; the first was, "You got the directions wrong." "Michael," I called, but the neighbor was far too distressed to brook interruption. "Too many trees," she wailed. My father was right—there were too many trees, the driveways were littered with debris, and I had to wait until every bit of it was gone before I could tell my husband that my father had died.

———

UNLIKE MY MOTHER, my father never wanted a house. When they married in 1942, he was a Merchant Marine whose possessions barely filled his small trunk. They took a room on Chicago's South Side; it had a bathroom down the hall, a hot plate for cooking, and a shelf in a refrigerator the tenants all shared. With my father on shore as little as four hours every three weeks, they didn't need more space. Often he didn't have time to come home, and my mother took the streetcar to meet him at Navy Pier. He was a wheelsman studying to

become a seaman third class, and though he'd been as far as Italy
and Honduras, after they married he mostly worked the Great
Lakes. He liked to be on the move. Though he had served for
a brief time in a CCC camp, he spent most of the Depression
years on the bum. Family travel, with two kids in the back seat
and a spouse in the front who could neither read a map nor fold
it, with expenses for restaurants and tourist homes, later motels,
never appealed to him, but the itinerary of his youth, the days of
hitchhiking and freight-hopping and working the boats, left an
impression as indelible as the anchor tattooed on his arm. He
had a remarkable sense of direction and never forgot an address,
astonishing my husband with his ability to recall the number of
the New Orleans rooming house on Dumaine or the flophouse
near the docks in San Francisco where he had spent a night nearly
sixty years before.

Although my mother was younger than my father, twenty-three
to his twenty-eight, by the time they married she had been on
her own nearly as long as he had. Her mother had died when she
was seven, leaving six children and a husband who would marry
twice more. Like her siblings she was put to work young—I don't
think any but the two youngest, adopted by my grandfather's
relatives in St. Louis and Albany, was allowed to finish school.
She cleaned rich people's houses, promising herself that when
she was grown she would have a house just like theirs, with a red
tile roof and oriental rugs. ("I was young," she says now with a
laugh. "What did I know?") Later she went to work in a cafeteria
in the shadow of the Sixty-third Street el. After her marriage,
which took place less than three months after Pearl Harbor, she
got a job in a defense plant and saved all her money. Still, given
my father's restlessness, had she and my father not had a family, I
don't think she would have gotten any house at all.

The family came as a surprise to my father, a bad case of
mumps in his teens having left him with the impression that
he was sterile, a secret he kept from my mother until she was

pregnant with me. From her point of view it was fortunate that I looked like him. He named me for his maiden aunt, his favorite aunt I was told (though to my knowledge he had no others) when at five I discovered my name on a tombstone in the cemetery in his Wisconsin hometown, Sturgeon Bay. I was an adult before my mother confided that he had been responsible for her death. She had been standing on the foyer rug when his grandparents' house caught fire, and when he snatched the rug to beat out the flames, she lost her balance, fell against the newel post, and broke her neck. My father died without knowing that I knew. He did not like children and hadn't wanted any, but he accepted my birth as a form of justice, a chance at expiation perhaps.

There was to be no such role for my brother, who was born just as the Great Migration of blacks from the South changed the color of Chicago's South Side. By then my father had left the Merchant Marines to take a job more suited to a man with a family, eventually going to work for Texaco, which had a storage facility in northern Indiana where my father loaded and unloaded the boats—only now do I realize they would have been tankers, for he never called them that. Everything from a skiff to a ship was a boat to him, as if that one word held a special kind of poetry, a poetry that single syllable still evokes for me. We were living in a one-bedroom walkup in Woodlawn, but with the arrival of my brother we needed more space.

"Get out of this neighborhood," shopkeepers advised my mother as all around us the buildings filled with black tenants and sold to black owners. Perhaps she thought my father would be pleased to live closer to his work, or maybe she was thinking about the fact that I was soon to start school. My mother tends to make decisions without consulting those they affect; even I, who love her, am frequently irked that she should be so overbearing. At any rate she had her brother drive her to

Hammond, Indiana, where she used the money she had saved
from the defense plant to make the down payment on a small,
two-bedroom frame house just going up on a tract of identical
half-built houses, and when my father came home from work,
surprised him with the news that he was a homeowner. I don't
think he ever forgave her.

Like every place I have lived in, that little gray house in
Hammond is coded into my memory by sound—the whoosh
of weatherstripping, sigh of plumbing, or creak of stair through
which I can reconstruct an entire building as well as the life
I lived there. It whispered worries: the rumor of a pipeline to
Alaska that would put my father out of work, the problem that
two bedrooms and two children of opposite genders would
eventually impose. The former made my parents cautious,
while the latter challenged their reluctance to make financial
commitments. My mother was in favor of adding on—not, she
was quick to point out, just an ugly ell out the back. She was
disdainful of the neighbors who had solved their similar dilem-
mas by tacking on a bedroom behind the kitchen. "It looks
like an addition," she would sniff, as if the offending wing had
been built for the sole purpose of displeasing her. On notebook
paper she had drawn up a design; she intended to supervise
the project herself. I should say here that the kitchen in this
house was very small; my six-foot father ate his dinner wedged
between the table and the stove. Supposedly he took one look
at the large but poorly planned kitchen of the house my mother
still lives in and said (uncharacteristically, for all his life he had
difficulty making decisions), "Let's buy this house." It was the
only house they looked at. The thought of my mother in charge
of a construction crew was, I think, too much for him to bear.

I am always amazed, when I go back to Hammond, how
shady that first neighborhood became, for when we moved
to that Levittown-like tract the ground was still so raw my

memory can barely plant it with grass. The new house too was in a tract, and I recall only two trees the entire length of the street, both in our yard, a big maple at the curb and a wild apricot in the back. The day we moved in a neighbor boy sassed my mother when she caught him climbing the maple and ordered him down, an incident that may have poisoned her attitude toward it. This summer the city is replacing the sidewalks along her street, and she's ecstatic that forty-four years later, it is at last marked with a big X for removal. Her feelings about the apricot were mixed. It was a beautiful tree, magical in the spring with its halo of delicately scented pale pink blossoms, and its fruit, smaller and more intensely flavored than the domesticated fruit one buys at the store, has rendered every apricot I've tasted since insipid. But much of the bounty wound up smeared on the sidewalk and the garage (those pesky neighborhood boys), and the tree drew bees. My mother was philosophical when my father "accidentally" fertilized it with weed killer and it eventually sickened and died.

It's astonishing that my father would have planted two other trees, both maples that were given to my mother as cherries— perhaps he was thinking of the orchards of his Wisconsin youth. The maple near the lot line never thrived, though it shed enough leaves every fall to irritate the neighbor, who repeatedly asked my now-divorced mother why the tree was there, to which she always replied, "Because Joe Ives put it there." Finally the neighbor asked if he could cut it down. The other grew to ninety feet, and for years my mother celebrated summer sitting in a lawn chair beneath it to "watch the leaves blow." But there were also leaves to rake and branches to trim, and if it ever fell, she fretted, it would fall on the house. The tree surgeon tried to talk her out of having such a healthy specimen taken down, but she grows petunias in tires on the stumps, as well as portulaca along the fence and impatiens in the shade of the garage. "Your father would never let me have flowers," she always points out. "He didn't want to mow around them when he cut the grass." Again she surveys her domain. Her house is so important to her that the first thing she did after they divorced was to redecorate every one of its five rooms so that her children could "know who I was." She was worried, she says, when she went on her own, but "I think the place looks better than it did when he was here." It's my cue to agree. In fact it does look better, and so I have to tell her she's right.

———

THE NOTE I FOUND in the strongbox on the floor of my father's closet concerned his house. It was not addressed, and there was no salutation or date. He may have written it moments or years before he took a blanket from his closet and his gun from its shelf and went into the backyard to end his life. Whichever, it was the only communication he left, and it said simply that it was his wish that Donna be allowed to remain in the house as long as she was able.

I found the note that Monday night after Donna and I returned from the cremation society, where I had signed the papers that authorized it to dispose of the body. A plane was to scatter his ashes over the Gulf of Mexico, and the society promised to send me a post card noting the date, time, latitude, and longitude, although two months later, when I called because the post card hadn't come, it couldn't find his record. I thought then of the one conversation we'd had about his plans. I had argued against them, in favor of a gravesite and memorial service, saying, "Don't you think I love you? Don't you think I'll miss you? Why do you want to just disappear?" It almost seemed ordained that five years later, when I needed one last death certificate to sell his house, I would call the Hernando

County Records Office and be told they had no record of him either.

Although my father's indecisiveness, his fear of making the wrong choice, often kept him from being a good planner, he was meticulously organized. An hour before he shot himself he sat down at the dining room table with Donna, writing out the checks to pay their bills. When she left for the beauty parlor, he kissed her and told her that he loved her. "I should have known then," she said to me later. He waited only long enough for her to have passed the bell tower at the entrance to High Point and turned onto Cortez Boulevard. It's surprising, his next-door neighbor says, that no one on the golf course would have heard the shot or seen the body, and perhaps it was his intent that some golfer spare Donna what she found when she came home at two. He tended to overlook contingencies and details. He forgot that I might already have left for the holiday weekend. He didn't think to take his wallet out of his back pocket. He left the note, an unofficial copy of his will, and the keys to his safe deposit box in his strongbox on the floor of his closet but failed to record the deposit box's new location when he changed banks.

Right key, wrong hole. I spent the next morning going from bank to bank until I found it. My father trusted no one; he held more than eighteen accounts at nearly a dozen banks. He bought stock and bonds acting as his own broker. Everything he owned, including his house, was in a living trust, for which I was now the trustee. Like many executors, I went into the job knowing nothing and was an expert by the next day. By the time I saw his lawyer that Friday, all the attorney had to do was record the quit-claim deed on the house where I was to maintain Donna.

I wished that he had just left it to her, of course. I liked Donna. I liked her spunk. Once when my father grumbled that he hoped he wouldn't live to be a hundred, she had informed

him that she not only planned to live that long, she intended
still to be dancing, a remark I recalled now with a sinking
heart. I didn't want the house; even more I didn't want to be
responsible for it. Did he think I would object if he left it to
her? I certainly didn't begrudge her the money he'd left her or
his car, the four-year-old white Crown Victoria I'd compli-
mented during his last trip to North Carolina. ("I decided
I wanted one more car before I died," he'd responded, then
frowned. "Sure seems like it got to be two years old mighty
fast." He traded cars every four years, so perhaps like Donna I
should have known then what was coming.) Already I could
feel the first throb of the headache that comes with owning
property out-of-state. It was the busiest week of the semester,
and in order to get back to my students, on the same Friday I
took possession I had to insure it, contract for pest control and
lawn care, change the utility accounts, arrange to pay the High
Point community dues, and list it with the county tax collector.
Scarcely a month of the next four years passed without a leak,
appliance failure, or worse. The central air had to be replaced;
a hurricane tore up the roof. The man who mowed the lawn
could never remember that I didn't live there, and every
time his invoice appeared in the mailbox, Donna panicked;
Terminix left notices of service she confused with bills. She
had difficulty keeping track of things. Over the four years that
she stayed on in the house I learned what a cruelty it would
have been for him to leave it to her. She was eighty-four when
my father died and though it wasn't yet evident already in the
first stage of Alzheimer's. She may yet live to be one hundred,
but she has forgotten how to dance.

I wish I believed that my father left the house to me out of
kindness to Donna, but he didn't want it to pass down to her
daughter and her daughter's children. It wasn't worth much,
but my father counted every penny. My accountant couldn't
understand why I couldn't find a copy of my father's last tax

return, but I *knew* why: he wouldn't have wanted to spend the ten cents on the copy machine. For years after their divorce, my parents quarreled about the house she still occupies, which had a year left on the mortgage when they split. "Your father didn't *give* me this house," she says at least once every visit. "We used the equity from the house on Oakdale to make the down payment, and we bought that house with the money I saved when I worked at the defense plant." He said, "I know one thing. No woman is ever going to throw me out of my own house again." She still says, "He was threatening me, so I got a restraining order, but I honestly thought he'd show up in court and call off the divorce."

Neither has ever admitted they divorced because they never got along, not for a day, not after my father left the boats and had to be home more than one afternoon every three weeks. I tiptoed through the small space of discord—the shouts, threats, and recriminations, an ongoing dirge driven by the occasional drum of physical blows. His relationship with Donna was less explosive, but the sound of their bickering no less constant. It floored him, he often told me, that with all the women around he could have picked out one "even more mule-headed than your mother." But his quarrels were not only with women. Toward the end of his life, he would have liked a reconciliation with my brother, though his way of asking for my brother's address was "Did your brother ever straighten himself out? What do you suppose his problem is anyway?" I would feel guiltier for not discerning what he wanted and putting them in touch if I didn't know that his way of making peace would have taken the very same tone.

My father was hard on everyone but hardest on my brother. During my brother's troubled adolescence, to get him away from my father, my mother sent him to a home for boys in Kansas. He finished school there, set out to see the West, and was arrested for possession of marijuana in Texas, where he spent over a year in jail waiting trial. To my father this proved what he'd known all along: my brother was no good. When my brother was younger the word my father used was *mistake*. (Throughout my childhood, whenever I looked up, he seemed to be staring. "Do you suppose you'll ever amount to anything?" he would ask, and when I answered, he always laughed as if to show he meant it as a joke, but the joke was on me, and his chuckle never masked the sound of a sneer.) My father forbade my mother any more contact with my brother. She arranged with her minister to receive letters at the church. She had a hysterectomy, and my father berated her as she left the recovery room. The minister recommended divorce.

The divorce went through. The pipeline went through, the Alaskan pipeline that had rumbled beneath the family melodrama until it became just another note in the score, part of the background shrill that was the sound two people seemed to make when they cried *wolf*. I'd stopped believing any of it long ago. My father was fifty-six, old enough to take early retirement, but he chose to start over, stoking furnaces and shoveling slag for Texaco's plant in Joliet for nine more years. My mother made the curtains for his apartment.

———

MY FATHER LIKED ATTENTION and was often perverse just to get it. Especially he liked the attention he commanded by threatening to die. Every Christmas he would ask my mother to take a "last picture" of him beside the Christmas tree, although he had nothing more seriously wrong with him than an ordinary case of lactose intolerance and his irritable bladder. When I was a senior in college, he was diagnosed with prostate cancer, though the surgeon who operated confided to my mother that he wasn't sure my father had the disease. He was seventy-eight before he developed angina. Yet he seemed convinced that he would die young (until it was too late for that, and then he was afraid he would die old), and his meager library was full of the various dictionaries of symptoms, treatment, and prevention that make up the hypochondriac's Bible. To me his obsession was, like the long-rumored pipeline, so much white noise; it lacked effect precisely because it was designed for one. He was fascinated with suicide, do-it-yourself euthanasia, and possessed a manual of methods that predated Jack Kevorkian's first book, though I'm not sure whether it was the fear of physical suffering or the financial loss of catastrophic illness that bothered him more. Three years before he died, on the only trip my husband made to my father's house, we were barely in the door before he brought his illustrated suicide guide to the table so that he could show his seven-year-old grandson how he planned to do it. My husband was horrified. We left the next morning, and he never went back.

Years later, when I drove from North Carolina to High Point for the last time, to ready my father's house for sale, as I came down the ramp from I-75 near Brooksville I found my way blocked by a SWAT team, squadrons of troopers, and more emergency and media vehicles than I had ever seen in one place. A gun fanatic named Hank Earl Carr, who had earlier that day killed his girlfriend's four-year-old son, two Tampa police officers, and a Florida state trooper, was inside the Shell station with a hostage. Later the hostage would report he'd promised that just before he killed himself he would let her go unharmed. Over and over he promised this was it, he was going to let her go "just as soon as I smoke this last cigarette." She said he seemed to be having a hard time working up his nerve, though by the time I reached the bell tower at High Point, Hank Earl Carr had pulled himself together and was dead.

"I'm not afraid to die," my father told his grandson as he spread his book on the table. I just didn't believe him. No matter what he said, when the time came I thought, like Hank Earl Carr, he would flinch.

My father arrived unexpectedly the last time he visited North Carolina. There was a knock at the door, and there he and Donna stood, suitcases in hand. "I told you we'd be up sometime this summer," he explained. He wouldn't say how long they planned to stay. That night we debated his final arrangements. It was probably the first time I told him I loved him, and when I got up the next morning he was already carrying their suitcases to the car. "But you just got here," I protested. They hadn't slept well, he said; the air-conditioning in their room was too cold. "I can turn it down," I pled. Besides, he said, he felt we had said everything that needed to be said the night before. "Anything else would just be loose chatter."

The last time I saw him we took my son fishing at a camp on the Weeki Wachi River not far from High Point. He gave Max his old red metal tackle box and told him that he believed Max had caught more fish in his ten years than he had in eighty. To me he volunteered that Michael and I had done a good job. It was as close as he ever came to telling me he loved me. It passed for a closeness between us, which turned out to be close enough.

Four autumns later, during the phase of discipline problems that accompanied my son's transition to high school, his guidance counselor called to tell me he had broken down in her office. My fourteen-year-old, six-foot-five-inch son, who at the time had brushed off all my attempts to discover how he felt about my father's death with a clipped shake of his head and "no big deal," had sobbed as he told her about his grandfather. It was horrible, she volunteered, referring to the suicide, but what she couldn't get over was that he had said, "My grandfather wasn't even a nice man, but he was nice to me, and I miss him."

She seemed shocked that anyone would say such a thing, and I had to tell her that the reason he said it was that it was true.

My father didn't feel good his last fall; he had no energy; he was slipping, Donna told me later. On the last morning of his life his doctor called. He had been in for a checkup, and the lab results were back; the doctor wanted him to report to the hospital that afternoon for more tests. I read the lab report, but the only thing it showed was that my father was anemic. He was afraid of cancer, but if that was the cause of the anemia the autopsy didn't find it. The only problem it noted was a gunshot wound to the head.

Donna didn't want an obituary for fear of being robbed, and though he would have liked one to appear in the Texaco bulletin, she was so adamant I allowed her to overrule me. And so there was no death notice, no service. I cleaned out his closet. The crematorium lost his ashes, and in the five years that passed before I sold his house, I misplaced my cache of death certificates only to be told that the Hernando County Office of Records had no record of his death. Still, I win. My father did not disappear. This is his record.

"YOU SHOULD BUY A HOUSE in Florida," my father liked to tell my mother when he went back north on visits. In turn she would mutter to me, "I should buy a house in Florida—I'd like to know where he thinks I'd get the money," and before I could point out that her house in Hammond was worth more than his, that she could in fact buy a house and retire to Florida if that was what she wanted, though we both knew it was not, she would be off and running: "You know he had more stock than he let on to my lawyer. Did I tell you he said your father was the most mercenary man he ever met?"

To both of my parents the house in Florida was not just a house but a symbol, and though its meaning was layered the bottom line was money, the final injustice or justice restored. And so when Donna's daughter, Juelane, called in the fall of 1997 to tell me her mother could no longer live alone, my first thought was to offer the house to my mother.

It was a stupid idea, of course. In the real world she would never consent to live in the house he had shared with "that old lady," a woman my mother never met but never refers to without contempt. Even if I'd come by the house by other means, if it had belonged to strangers, my mother is, if anything, even less a joiner than my father was; I can't imagine her taking line dancing or ceramics; she would refuse to attend High Point's dinner dances or share a table at the Sunday breakfasts in the golf club's bar and grill. She would complain that the men were all bald and had potbellies; nor would she care to know the women gabbing away their afternoons at the pool. She's rooted to her house in Hammond and those who remain of her original neighbors; she would never move to Florida no matter how much she frets about shoveling snow. Even as a symbolic gesture I would have gotten it all wrong. "The house is not the point," she would have answered, disappointed that I could forget the house in Hammond is a symbol too.

The following summer, when the realtor had an offer, I dug through the papers I'd filed away when I finished my father's estate four years before. I found the quit-claim deed, but not the titles. They looked like car titles, the realtor told me, and I needed one for each half of the house. And though I ought to have cried—I had never seen them; I had no idea where to look—I laughed. "You mean to tell me," I said, "that I own my father's house *in halves*?" And so, in the end, I suppose you could say that his house became a symbol to me too.

———

IF YOU FOLLOW CORTEZ BOULEVARD west from High Point to the intersection with US 19 at Weeki Wachee and go straight, you will find yourself on county road 550. A few miles farther, a fork to the right will take you to the beach at Pine Island, but if you stay on 550 at the end of the road you will come to a dot on the map called Bayport. It is not a town, just two or three houses and then a short tunnel of live oak and Spanish moss that opens into a small park where the land meets the Gulf of Mexico. This is the mouth of the Weeki Wachee River. A historical marker discloses that the village of Bayport sprang up as a port in the 1850s, after central Florida was opened to white settlers at the end of the Second Seminole War. During the Civil War, when Union forces blockaded the larger ports, the Weeki Wachi became an important trade route, and it remained Hernando County's major outlet until the railroad reached Brooksville in 1885. Now there is no echo of commerce, only the occasional fisherman motoring by, a splash of mergansers, the drill of a red-bellied woodpecker, and chattering of blackbirds in the sabal palms. On a calm morning, when the sea is a pastel glass, the red and green triangles of the channel markers recede into a distance that vanishes into sky at the horizon. To the east, behind a tidal canal, spreads the spartina grass of the marsh, broken in the middle distance by a small hammock of palms, an island in a golden sea whose far shore is a dark wood of oak, palmetto, and pine. And if you did not remember that beyond that dense wood, six miles to your past, lay the strip malls and franchises of the working-class Midwest's retirement heaven, you could believe in the endlessness that is renewal.

I came here first with my father, at the end of the tedious day that included my father's presentation of his suicide book to my son and a visit to Rogers' Christmas House, a complex of bric-a-brac shops that the men took one look at and fled, seeking refuge on the porch and occasioning a squabble between Donna and my father, who was miserable with the host's task of trying to find something everyone would enjoy. In the soft light of early evening, standing on the pier that overlooks the marsh to one side and the Gulf of Mexico to the other, I was stunned to discover such beauty in a place where I had believed there was none. It is the place to which I returned all that week after my father died and again that next January, when I came back to Florida, the place where I came to grieve, though I cannot say whether it was my father's death or his life that I grieved for.

I came back there again the last winter I owned my father's house, when I came to get it ready for my tenants, the only week out of the years the house was under my care that I came to feel that I owned it, when I slept not as a guest but in the big master bedroom that had been Donna's, laying claim to the possession that resides in solitude. Every morning of that week I rose before dawn and drove the ten miles to Bayport through a thick fog that began the other side of US 19, as if in crossing that highway I had crossed into another world. By the time I arrived, the fog would have begun to lift with first light, and I could just see the gathering of egrets and great blue herons come to feed along the canal. It is like a snowstorm, that light in which everything is muted. There are shades but no color, and in that early hour that wraps the land in a veil of bridal vapor, heaven and earth are wedded inside its frail gauze of light. The world reveals itself slowly, first the water below me, then the shapes of the land, the tufts of cedars, and finally the faint silhouette of palms. Later, when the rising sun spangled the last webs of mist that clung to the marsh, I drove back to High Point to take up my chores for the day. In the late afternoon I returned to watch the golden grass deepen to amber as the shadow of the coming evening began to creep from the edge of the marsh to its far shore. Each night a lone egret landed in the top of a pine just across the channel, standing sentinel as the solid blue of the sky dissolved into the delicate palette that is not sunset but the eastern sky's intimation of it, until at last the sun sank behind the palms on the island across from the pier. There was nowhere I would rather have been.

But in May, when I came back to High Point for the last time, it wasn't the same. At my invitation Juelane, who had come to help me clean out the house, slept in the big bedroom that had, after all, been her mother's, and I retreated to my father's cramped one, the one I'd occupied as her mother's guest. Already the air was unbearably heavy, and in the mornings we walked the loop of High Point Boulevard before the day's heat made exercise imprudent; in the evenings we went out to eat. I didn't return to Bayport until I'd driven her to the Tampa airport, the day before I would leave. Even in the early morning, the veils of mist and birds were gone. I'd brought camera equipment, but the air was so thick with heat and bugs that after the fewest of minutes I put my tripod away. It didn't matter. The haze ruined the light anyway.

It was a year of drought, the worst Florida wildfires in history, and though the air was sodden, the land was parched. In my yard the grass crackled beneath my feet. I would have watered, but what was the point? As soon as I left it would just turn brittle again. There was no reason to visit the nursery, though in the backyard where my father died, in spite of everything, I had wanted to plant a tree.

Later that summer the realtor would find a buyer; I would find the death certificate I needed at the Hernando County Department of Health instead of the Records Office and the titles to the two halves of the house in the bottom of an accordion file tucked away in my attic, and sign the whole over to another Midwesterner in search of the land his lifetime of labor had promised.

On the last morning I spent in my father's house, I washed my sheets and towels so that I could leave them folded in the linen closet, Juelane having decided to sell the furnishings with the house. As I waited for them to dry, I brought a stool to take a last inventory of the shelves my father installed below the roof of the laundry shed. Years ago I'd taken home the tools Donna wanted to sell, just as she'd wanted to sell the clothes I gave to Goodwill, the dusty bottle of scotch, and fatal .357 Bulldog revolver, but there were still drawers full of neatly sorted washers and screws that the realtor advised me to leave in case the new owner was handy. A fan, a cooler, a Coleman lamp. Satisfied I'd left nothing I shouldn't, I was about to climb down when I saw it, wedged beneath the eave at the far back of the shelf. It was my father's old seaman's trunk, the one that had once housed everything he owned. I reached, but the stool was wobbly; I was afraid I would fall. The trunk was too far back and probably too heavy. So I left it. I took the sheets from the dryer, put them away, and locked the door.

A STONE'S WEIGHT

———

I.

My mother was seven years old and already in the Chicagoan Home for Orphans when her mother died. My grandmother's family had not approved of the penniless and irascible red-headed Irishman she married, and though they had her body shipped home to St. Louis, they cut all ties to her children and buried her in an unmarked grave. Neither my mother nor any of her brothers and sisters ever saw their mother's family again.

My mother wants me to know this story, although her childhood is not really a story she tells, but a jumble of details she is forever reassembling. "Seniors," she says. "We don't have a future. All we have is a past." And so again and again we work her past as if it is a puzzle.

She was the fourth of the six children my grandmother left behind. The oldest was named for her mother: Cresenthia, or perhaps it was Crysenthia; my mother doesn't know how it was spelled. Like her mother she was called Centa, and in the few photographs of my grandmother one can identify them as mother and daughter by the same plain Germanic features and lank hair. Centa was thirteen, Eleanor eleven, my Uncle Bud nine, Tommy three, and Ruth nearly one. Sometimes my mother says there must have been another child between her and Tommy, though she has no recollection of the child or its death. Other times she tells me she had a brother who lived only a few days.

Although my grandmother was not yet thirty-two when she died, she had been sick for a long time, and she asked my grandfather's brother Tom and his wife Laura in Albany to promise that they would take Ruth, who was in her teens before she learned that they weren't her real parents; she overheard a conversation between her aunts, but blamed my mother because she was afraid to blame an adult, something that nagged at her conscience even past middle age, when she and my mother discovered a need to reconnect as sisters. Three-year-old Tommy was adopted by my grandfather's sister Molly in St. Louis. But my grandfather apparently got along with his own family no better than he had with his first wife's, and my mother was in her forties before she met her brother Tom.

"I don't remember either Tommy or Ruth as children," she says.

"Well, you must have known Ruth," I say. "You told me she blamed you for telling her she was adopted."

"She did," my mother replies. To her the story is perfectly clear. The inconsistencies I stumble over do not exist.

The second child, Eleanor, also went to St. Louis, where she stayed with my grandfather's other sister, and in exchange for her board helped raise her aunt's children. Centa quit school and went to work, which left my mother and Bud, the middle children, the ones who were, in my mother's words, "too old to be cute and too young to be useful." Sometime before their mother died my grandfather boarded them out, but the caretaker abandoned them, and they were sent to the Chicagoan Home, where they remained until their father remarried the following year.

"Centa stole her milk—you know, the woman my father hired to board us, so we got sent to the home. My mother arranged for us to stay at St. Mary's." So she was in St. Mary's Episcopal Home when her mother died? I ask. My mother's voice stains with impatience. "The Chicagoan Home, I told you. Centa was there too. She had to work in the kitchen and take care of the little kids." She pauses and adds, "At St. Mary's." It irritates her that I can't get this straight. She wants me to know her.

My mother has a single memory of her mother, a vague recollection of seeing her fall out of a chair. Though officially my grandmother died of pneumonia, the real illness went undiagnosed. "In those days they didn't know," my mother says to me, adding with characteristic emphasis, "they just didn't."

For a while she was convinced her mother died of pernicious anemia. Over the course of my life I have heard theories of tuberculosis, multiple sclerosis, heart trouble, cancer. Only recently my mother confided that her mother was losing the use of her extremities and had trouble keeping her tongue in her mouth, details I'm glad she did not divulge before, for I can well imagine the portrait of my grandmother that lolling tongue would have inspired in a child.

"They told me she had to chew gum," my mother reported to a doctor who took her family history a few years ago. "Diabetes," he guessed, and now my mother says, almost proudly, "I have diabetes in my family."

She is waiting to inherit it. It would give her a connection to her mother.

Although nearly everything my mother knows about her mother would have come from Eleanor or Centa, and more likely Eleanor—for it was their habit to quarrel about their parents whenever she and my mother got together during Eleanor's last years—it is possible that it was Ruth, the youngest sister, who divulged their mother's symptoms. Centa and Eleanor have been dead for years, and what they could remember my mother and Ruth shared a need to reconstruct. Ruth might even have had the advantage, for once the secret of her birth was out, my great uncle and aunt might have been willing to pass along what they knew about her mother. Nothing my mother knows came from her father. She was afraid to ask questions, for questions betrayed ignorance, and "my father didn't want dumb kids."

Only once did she inquire about her family; within earshot of her stepmother she inquired when they were "going to get Ruthie back." Whether he would have told her anything had his new wife been less volatile I can't say. He may have thought there was no point. Though we lived only a few miles away, first in Chicago, then in Hammond, Indiana, I saw him no more than a handful of times in the seven years that our lives overlapped. When my mother asked why he wouldn't come to see us, he responded, "Too many stoplights." On the single visit he did make to Hammond, she took pains to bake him an apple pie, for he had been especially fond of his second wife's apple pie—which wasn't very good according to my mother, who both hated her stepmother and prided herself on her pies. He refused to taste it, and though her feelings were crushed, she tells the story with relish, as if to boast, "That's my dad!" Bull-headed is the term she uses to describe him, and she prides herself on her bullheadedness every bit as much as her pies.

His second wife, Maud, was a Harvey Girl. A traveling insurance salesman, he met her at a train station, and his family believed that he was carrying on with her before my grandmother died, perhaps one of the reasons their relationship with him soured. Not so, says my mother, adamant that he did not meet Maud until after, although it was from her that I derived my childhood impression that my grandfather was off chasing another woman when his wife died. "My father was a marrying man," my mother used to say, for by the time I was born Maud had died and he had taken a third wife, Etta. I'm not sure whether it was Eleanor's death, my brother's third marriage, or my second that ushered in the revised history, which has become, now that Eleanor is no longer around to correct her, a work-in-progress, ever improving.

"There was no love there," she insists of her father and Maud, whom she and Bud called Ma. Maud looks like a Ma in my mother's pictures, white-haired, heavy-breasted, stout through the middle, dressed in the shapeless cotton housedresses, rolled stockings, and sturdy black lace-up shoes of the time. Older than my grandfather—even older than she let on, my mother says with some anger—she had two adult daughters and a son. My grandfather married her, my mother maintains, solely to get a home for his children. "So why did she marry him?"

"To get a home for her children," my mother repeats in an overly matter-of-fact tone.

"Her children were grown." I can't seem to follow the story in the way that she wants.

But in those days children lived at home until they married, no matter their age; so Maud's daughter, Josephine, and son, Ed, who had syphilis and later died in an insane asylum, lived with them free, though at fourteen my aunt Centa had to pay room and board. When Josephine married the iceman, Maud stole Centa's shoes and gave them to her daughter. When my mother got a new dress, Maud presented it to Josephine before my mother could wear it; whenever my mother earned money, she had to turn it over to Ed. After school she washed walls and did the housework, or else she was sent to Maud's daughter Mame's to clean; then, after supper, when the other children had gone in from play, Maud turned her out to get some fresh air, and she huddled on the cold stoop in the dark until she was allowed to come in at nine. Still, on the night of her stepmother's death my mother claims she woke to hear Maud calling, "Dorothy, Dorothy," which is strange, not because of the claim to clairvoyance—for by then my mother, whose name is Dorothine and not Dorothy, a distinction no one including my father seemed to recognize, had quit school, gone to work, and was no longer living at home—but because she remembers her stepmother with such staunch lack of affection. Yet who else would there have been for Maud to appeal to? Josephine had run off with another man, both Mame and Ed were sick, and my grandfather was apparently not the sort of man you could count on when you were dying. Perhaps Maud understood that, having been left by her mother too young, my mother would abandon no one.

When my mother was thirteen or fourteen Josephine's husband and Ed began to "look at her funny," and as she ripened into the prettiest of the four Hurley girls—the smallest and darkest of hair, she points out in her album, the girl her father called their "little Irish beauty," the one she now claims he told her was most like her mother—Josephine grew jealous and Maud's temper worse. My mother saw Mame's house as a refuge until her husband made a pass. After that my mother tried to avoid him, Maud beat her for shirking, and Mame's demeanor toward her chilled.

They were poor, and then the Depression came, and they were hungry.

"I used to think how worried my father looked sitting in his wing chair with his feet on his footstool," my mother says. "He must have been scared to death." Once she stole an orange from the grocer. "I bet you choked on it," I say, surprised my mother would admit to theft, for she is honest to a fault, the fault being pride, as proud of her scruples as she is of her bull-headedness and her pies. "I bet you couldn't even swallow it," to which she replies, "It was the best orange I ever ate." When there was food, her stepmother ruled the table with a waste-not-want-not rigor that left my mother incapable of expressing her food phobias in an adult, which is to say polite, manner; at eighty-six she still makes faces and rude sounds at the mere mention of anything she dislikes. Across the country there are waiters who know what my mother was forced to eat as a child.

They moved a lot, though never far from Sixty-third Street on Chicago's South Side. "I suppose we got evicted," she says. On Saturdays she and her brother patrolled the alleys for fuel. At night they opened the door of their flat to use the light from the hall. Her stepmother sent her to make excuses to the butcher and the grocer. Once, when she was on her way home with Centa's board money, a man jabbed a gun in her back.

"I ran like hell," she says. "I was more afraid to come home without the money than I was to be shot."

"I didn't have a childhood, not really," she says, but I am witness to the fact that she had two: the one that began in 1925, the year of her mother's death, the one in which she was always cold, hungry, neglected, resented, and abused—the one she remembers—and the other one, the one that ended the year the other began, the perfect one she was too young to remember and so is doomed to invent.

2.

ALTHOUGH THERE ARE PICTURES of my grandmother with Centa, Eleanor, and Bud, there are no pictures of her with my mother. The only picture of my mother as a child is a snap-shot of the four oldest siblings in which she is a baby. Centa and Eleanor stand behind the cart in which she sits, looking much as I remember them as adults—Centa squinting into the camera with her earnest face and straight, skinned-back hair, Eleanor sharp-faced and preening beneath a long mane of red curls. My uncle Bud, whom I never knew in any incarna-tion but rail-thin and bald, is here a chubby, cotton-haired tot who has my mother locked around the neck in a clumsy bear hug. My mother wears bloomers and dark leggings; her head is turned to the side, and in the faded light it is impossible to make out her features.

For years the photograph has hung on my dining room wall in a collection of old photos. When I take it down, it falls out of its frame, and the oval mat comes loose. Behind the mat, in the background, I discover a man. He is standing on a sidewalk with his back to the camera. There is no way to know if he is my grandfather. But he has his back to the children.

As a girl, my mother was close to Centa and Bud. When Bud took a job selling ice cream from a freezer he wore on his back, he bought my mother a diamond ring with his first paycheck. I've had it sized to fit my little finger, a chip set in a square of white gold intended to make the tiny stone look larger. It pleases my mother to have me wear it, but it cannot mean to me what it does to her, even more than the engage-ment ring my father gave her, both commitments she took as binding, though it was only a matter of time before the brother would buy another girl a diamond and be gone.

He and Centa married the same year, just as nearly half a century later they would die the same year. Bud was twenty. His bride's name was Joan, and she looked just like Joan Baez, though her voice was hardly a pure soprano. A fastid-ious housekeeper who kept see-through plastic jackets on the furniture, and opened her cabinets with a dish towel to prevent fingerprints, she hated dirt but loved dirty jokes, which she told with a raucous cackle that erupted into a long spurt of randy laughter. Once I got sick while we were at my aunt Joan's, and because her father was in the bathroom, I had to vomit in the kitchen sink while Joan wrung her dish towel in the doorway and wailed, "Oh my God, oh my God."

Her father, a small, dark Syrian who never said a word, lived in the back bedroom, an arrangement she must have begrudged, for my uncle often told her, "Never you mind, Joannie, when he dies that room's going to make you a nice den."

"Bud and Joan had a beauty-ful marriage," my mother always says. They were sweethearts, and though Joan was somewhat contemptuous of the Hurleys—the snide jocularity with which she pronounced the name never failed to jerk my mother to her feet and send her out the door—my mother has passed scarcely a week of the decades since Bud died without a letter from Joan bewailing her loss. She made a brief second marriage to a man who helped her dust my uncle's gravestone every day but divorced him when she discovered that all the polishing in the world would not shine him up into her Johnny. For a while, when that second marriage was breaking up, she seemed to write every day, but no matter how lugubrious her letters, my mother answered every one because, "Say what you will about Joan, she made my brother very happy."

Centa's groom was a divorcé named Ernest Magnotti, who had a great, husky hee-hee of a laugh and hair as black and shiny as patent leather. Ernie was Catholic; so their wedding had to take place in City Hall, but the marriage lasted nearly fifty years. On the day of my own second marriage, my mother called just as the ceremony was scheduled to start to tell me that Ernie had a stroke. Every Sunday from then until his death my mother, who never drove on highways, traveled the back roads from Hammond to the far southwest corner of Chicago in order to take Centa to visit him in the nursing home. He no longer knew his wife and was often abusive, but every weekday and Saturday Centa rode a bus to see him, a round trip involving two transfers and four hours. After he died their son moved her to Texas, where she grieved to be so far from the grave. That summer she took a Greyhound bus to Hammond to say goodbye to my mother. She had an aneurism but wasn't strong enough to survive surgery. "She doesn't want it anyway," my mother said. "She wants to be with Ernie."

"Centa had a hard life," my mother says now. "Ernie had a temper. She adored him, and oh, I guess he loved her all right, but I don't think she had it as good as she wanted people to think."

It's news to me—Ernie was my favorite uncle, and more than once after her divorce I heard my mother complain to Centa, "I wish I'd had a husband who talked nice like that to me. I don't know what it feels like to have someone think you're special." Invariably Centa changed the subject.

It's true that my mother's marriage—to a poor and irascible red-headed man who had trouble getting along with others—turned out badly. My father didn't talk much and saw no reason that anyone else should either. My mother is a talker, though she needs far too much from conversation to be successful at it. It is not possible for her to listen to others, and her words are freighted with appeals for pity and invitations to praise that embarrass and wear at the nerves and only guarantee that others will disappoint her. "I thought I was going to be so happy," she says bitterly to me. "He was tall and had broad shoulders and auburn hair. I thought the sun rose and set on him." No doubt she believed that when she wed her real life would begin, that the family she created would cancel out the one she lost. Perhaps she even thought my father would prove a kindred spirit. His mother too died when he was young, but I never heard him mention her, not once, and the only thing I know about his mother is that he did not like her.

If I am surprised to hear my mother acknowledge that Centa "didn't have it so good," for I know all too well her tendency to idealize the marriages of others in order to bemoan the defects of her own, I am also struck by what she does not say: that whatever disappointments Centa's marriage may have held, she was bonded to Ernie and had no need to air them. Bud rarely spoke to anyone but Joan, and though my mother and Centa could share an occasional laugh about their childhood dog, Spotty, or Dickie, the canary who loved only my grand-father but could not abide his hat, or the time their father and his poker pals sent them out for sandwiches and they used the money to go to the show, they never talked about what they lost when their mother died. "I wish I had picked Centa's brain," my mother says now, and when I ask why she didn't, she says, "The opportunity never came up." No, I think, it wouldn't have. My mother might have survived the harsh childhood or comfortless marriage, but the combination scarred her with an insecurity so relentless and deep that neither her brother nor her sister had the power or volition to tend it.

Although she lived three hundred miles away, it was inevita-ble that my mother would turn to Eleanor, who was widowed around the same time my parents divorced. Eleanor had been nearly forty when she married, and none of us went to her wedding, which she resented. She sent stacks of pictures, so many that Joan, who observed that Eleanor had photographed everything else, wondered why she'd left out the wedding night.

"I had two little kids. How was I supposed to go?" my mother protests to me now, though according to her that's something else Eleanor resented. Eleanor never had children.

"She was just bitter," my mother says, "a bitter old woman. She was my sister, and I loved her, but God she gave me a hard time. If I said something was white she would say it was black. I don't know why she had to be so contrary."

Other times she says, "They brainwashed her," meaning the St. Louis aunts, the sisters my grandfather's second wife sent packing. Eleanor too believed my grandfather was carrying on with Maud before their mother died, and she blamed the death on my grandfather's philandering and habit of procreation.

"Women had a lot of kids in those days. They all did," my mother says, her voice rising as if in Eleanor's absence she will continue the dispute with me. "You can't blame my dad."

She and my mother began to visit, but Eleanor found fault with everything: the light in my mother's bathroom wasn't bright enough; the restaurants around Hammond were no good. Invariably my mother, who rarely drinks, would choose a family-style place, and Eleanor, who liked a cocktail with dinner, would spend the meal complaining.

"I told her, 'Eleanor, where you come from it may be different, but around here restaurants just don't serve alcohol,'" my mother reports, which is, of course, untrue. My mother simply doesn't know the ones that do, which was another thing that grated on Eleanor, my mother's reluctance to venture beyond the tried and true.

To my mother differences in taste are not matters of preference but marks of character, which is for her the measure of success. One of the reasons she and my father fared so poorly together is that for him the measure was money. She boasts of her independence and resilience; there was nothing my father valued less in a woman. "Eleanor was vain," my mother says now. "Always dressed up like a Christmas tree. I couldn't believe it when she came to our father's funeral wearing all that black eye makeup. She looked like a raccoon. And she thought I was terrible because *I* didn't wear lipstick." Eleanor was fancy; my mother is plain. Eleanor liked soap operas; my mother can't stand them. Eleanor played bingo; my mother refused to go. Year after year Eleanor tried to get my mother to accompany her to Vegas. They did go to Mackinac Island—via Detroit because Eleanor wouldn't listen when my mother read the highway signs. My mother packed a picnic, but Eleanor refused to stop. There was nothing they didn't quarrel about. It made her mad, Eleanor said, that my mother sent me to college but not my brother, no matter how many times my mother told her that my brother didn't want to go. The real issue, my mother says, was that she had children and Eleanor didn't. The real issue, she says, was that Eleanor resented her and Bud because their father got them out of the orphanage after he remarried. "What did she want? My father sent her ten dollars for bus fare. She wouldn't come." "I didn't want to come," Eleanor told her.

This is, of course, my mother's side of the story. I can guess at Eleanor's. To her my mother was too retiring, too timid, too unwilling to get out and have some fun. After my parents divorced my mother refused to attend Parents Without Partners or any other singles' events, saying the men would all be bald and the women would be hostile; they didn't want the competition. "No," she would say, "I'm happy like I am." After the fractious twenty-eight years of her marriage, what my mother craved was peace, a state Eleanor found boring.

My mother has her own resentments. Eleanor knew the St. Louis family, the aunts and cousins my mother would have liked to know. "You wouldn't believe I'm from a big, close family, but I am. Do you know at Eleanor's wake I saw a little kid, some third or fourth cousin, reach out to touch her hand?" Eleanor got to have a relationship with their brother Tom. "We were just kids," she says. "It wasn't fair to punish us just because the adults couldn't get along."

Eleanor was old enough to remember their mother.
What Eleanor wanted from my mother was a pal, a traveling companion, but the only place my mother really wanted to go was home, and what she wanted from Eleanor was collaboration. "When my mother was alive, we always had the biggest Christmas tree on the block," she used to tell me. "My mother could play piano by ear. My mother made her own wedding dress. My mother was a very talented woman." She worships her mother and idolizes her father. How it must have galled Eleanor to listen. It was Maud, not her father, who quarreled with his sisters, according to my mother. *Her* father was a family man. "My father loved us," my mother insists, demonstrating how he used to pass a penny behind his back for her to buy a Mary Jane. "You wouldn't expect a man to be sensitive, but my father was. He appreciated art." I know the catalogue by heart, because, unlike the bad childhood, the details of the good childhood never vary: He loved pretty china; he listened to opera on the radio; he took them to the Art Institute. Once he drove them to the site of the Valentine's Day Massacre and told them, "This is the underworld." "We hadn't gone under anything. I couldn't figure out what he meant, but I wasn't going to ask, not and have my father think I was *stupid*. My father was a brilliant man," my mother says. "I always thought it was a shame he didn't have an education. He would have made a good lawyer." This last, I presume, because he liked to argue.
"The old man was a son-of-a-bitch," Eleanor said.

3.

NO DAUGHTER COULD have cherished my mother enough.
When I was small, if I didn't come the instant I was called, she threatened to leave me; whenever I displeased her, she stopped speaking. Well into her seventies she still threatened to leave my house at the least disappointment. Throughout my

adulthood she has scripted conversations in her head, growing morose when I fail to deliver my lines. She tells me when to call my brother and what to say; once, when I objected, she grew so angry she vowed I would never hear from her again. For a month she wrote letters detailing my crimes, a list that grew longer with each letter and went back to babyhood. "This is the last you will ever hear from me," she insisted in every one, signing herself "the old witch in Hammond." But of course it wasn't. She couldn't let me go.

As a teen, I chafed under her protection. She could not permit me to hang out with friends; she was afraid they might stop at a drive in for hamburgers. "You know that kind of food isn't well balanced," she cried. "You think these people are your friends, but they don't care about your health." In college when she came to visit she did not want to meet my friends. She still prefers not to meet them. It bothers her that I have friends. They compete with her for my attention.

When she visits, she sits between my husband and me on the sofa. Years ago, as I graduated from college, she was furious because I looked at my fiancé instead of her; on our first visit home after our wedding, she burst into our bedroom at dawn because she couldn't wait any longer to see which nightgown I was wearing. Later, when I finally told her I had left him and was living with the man who would become my second husband, the first thing she said, was, "Have you told him about me?" I laughed. "What about you?" I said. "You know. What I'm like." She had a list of characteristics she wanted me to convey. *Independent. Resourceful. Creative.* Neither *controlling* nor *possessive* was on it.

Only recently has she begun to make or receive weekend visits. "If you can't give me a week of your time, I don't want to see you at all," she used to say, by which she meant nine days, for by her definition a week includes both weekends. During my senior year in college she got the dates of spring break mixed up, and when I didn't show up on time rather than calling me and discovering her error, she called the police. Once I stopped in Bloomington, Indiana to do some research at my alma mater on my way to Hammond, and when I discovered that the morning bus didn't run on Sunday, that I would have to wait till afternoon, she refused to believe me and insisted I was trying to shortchange her. The following year, when I taught at a writers' conference in Sioux City, Iowa, and arrived at the airport for my flight to Chicago only to be told that the airline had sold me a bad ticket, that the flight I had booked did not run on weekends, I made the airline call my mother.

Tell them your mother *has priority*, she likes to say. *Your mother says so.* And, *I know these things, I'm a mother*, even though for more than two decades I have been one too.

When my son was born, she came to help, but her flight was delayed until 2 a.m., and my husband picked her up at the airport while I dozed on the sofa between feedings. A few minutes later she was at the door, saying, "I've had a horrible day, and I'm hungry. What are you going to feed me?" She likes for me to feed her. When she asks if she can help it is always as we sit down to the table. "You should make it easy for yourself and fix something we can eat again tomorrow," she suggested shortly after my C-section, but while she was helping my husband clean up she got so involved in talking to him she dropped the vegetables on the floor and left the roast on the counter overnight. Once, when Max was a toddler, I asked her to watch him while I cooked, and while she was busy talking to me he fell down the stairs.

When I sat on the sofa to breastfeed, she sat beside me to talk, leaning so close I wound up with my back arched over the arm, my infant son screaming. "You must not have enough milk" was her interpretation. When I tried to nurse behind the closed door of my bedroom, she pushed it open and perched beside me on the bed. She wanted to buy her grandson a playpen but waited until he was fed to take a bath and get dressed; by the time we reached the store he was hungry again. Horrified, she snapped, "You wouldn't have this problem if you bottle-fed." When I went to my six-week checkup she complained I was gone too long. He hadn't cried, but what would she have done if he had?

"After all," she said, "I don't have what it takes to feed him."

Only later did she confide that she had wanted to breastfeed herself, but after my brother was born she had an infection, and "you," she said, "you just stiffened up and wouldn't take my nipple."

For years I stiffened up. My mother is exhausting. She's manipulative; her need for attention is relentless. She is also funny, generous, and loving. When I wanted to go to college and my father refused to send me, she went to work in a school cafeteria in order to pay my tuition and board. I could never forget this. Every time I see her she reminds me.

But now she is eighty-six, the only parent my husband and I have left, and the ruthless hand of time is weighing on her shoulders, shattering her teeth, and weakening her heart. It is no longer I who am leaving her, but she who is leaving me. Her hold on me has relaxed because she is loosening her hold on the earth, and though I have stores of patience now, it makes no difference that I did not discover them sooner, for I took the message of her training, her angry silences and threats, much too literally. Her love was not conditional at all. No mother's love could have been more unconditional. I know her even better than she wanted.

All children commit the same crime: they grow up to become their own person. And because my son is twenty-one, I know now that it is as hard to let go as it is to break free. How could I have expected my mother to understand my need to leave? I have the one thing she would have given anything for: I have a mother.

4.

THERE IS A FAMILY STORY: on her deathbed, my grandmother escaped from the hospital, came home, and looked through the window to see how her children were doing; she couldn't die without making sure they were all right. It is not certain which of the children first told it. At some point each of them probably came to believe that he or she was the one to look up and see their mother's face at the glass. The image is frozen in my mother's mind, her mother outside the window, hair wild, in the dark the long cotton nightgown and bare feet a ghostly white, though the truth is that by then there was no home, the children were scattered, and my mother admits that the only memory she has of her mother is of her falling out of a chair, and even that she's not sure about—"Maybe," she says wistfully, "someone just told me." Still she believes her mother came home. It's the central myth of the happy childhood memory has denied her. One of the children must have dreamed it; they all would have believed it because they needed to. When I was younger I believed it too. I probably added the bare feet, long white nightgown, and wild hair.

This is what I have to construct a grandmother from: a little bit of lace she tatted, her autograph album, and five photographs.

The lace my mother removed from two threadbare pillowcases and used to edge pillows she made for my living room.

"I always wonder what she was thinking while she made that lace," my mother muses. "If she made it while she was waiting to get married or to have one of her children. I always wonder if she might have made it while she was expecting me."

It is the lace that convinces my mother her mother was artistic, by which she means romantic too, for she has endowed my grandmother with her own temperament. In her eyes my grandmother is at once a dreamy girl and perfect mother, instead of a girl who became a woman too young, whose life after marriage surely didn't match her dreams, who became sick and wore herself out giving birth to and caring for six children.

Dear Centa:

The world is filled with flowers,
The flowers are filled with dew,
The dew is filled with love for you for you for you.

Your friend,
Frank Moehsmer
October 19, 1909

My grandmother was fifteen years old when those lines were written in her album. Little more than a year later she married my grandfather, and ten months after that she gave birth to my Aunt Centa.

Man's love is like Scotch snuff
You take a pinch and that's enough:
Profit by this sage advice.
When you fall in love think twice.

Maybell Brown
October 16, 1909

My mother has given me the book, covered in decaying waxed brown paper. *Sweethearts Always* it is titled, *Poems of Love*, for dreamy girls waiting to become perfect wives and mothers, its first eighteen pages "embellished with Cupids, Hearts and Flowers along with mottoes of the sort that were in olden times engraved on engagement or wedding rings." "After-Consent-Ever-Content," they promise, and though the preface warns that the Literature of Love is so voluminous "it would seem that no novelty of poetic expression were left the modern lover," presumably the hundred blank pages that followed were an invitation to try. But the canned verses penned by schoolmates in the spidery, formal handwriting of the time reveal more about the era than about my grandmother or their authors. In heavily bedizened letters my grandmother inscribed the flyleaf:

> To write in my album
> I kindly invite
> But tearing out pages
> I call Impolite.

They are the only surviving words in her hand.

Most of the names signed in the album are German; her parents' names were Frank Vogler and Minnie Schultz. The only thing I really know about my grandmother is that she must have come from St. Louis' sizeable German middle class.

That she was middle class I assume from her wedding portrait, which is full of the pretentious studio props and backdrops of the time: faux window with heavy draperies and painted ivy; a mirror with a massive, elaborately carved frame; an ornate pedestal on which the maid of honor rests her hand. The picture was taken in 1911, when long exposures would have required that subjects hold stiffly still, and perhaps that explains why all stare at the camera without smiling. The groom and his best man wear dark suits, shiny dress shoes, boutonnieres, and white ties. The maid of honor is attired in a demure ankle-length white dress with a yoke piped in ball fringe; she wears pearls and white high-heeled slippers. Cradled in one arm is a bouquet of white roses; another rose is fastened to one side of her cloud of dark Gibson-Girl hair. My grandmother's dress has a high neck, three-quarter sleeves, and an hourglass bodice that would have been shaped by an undergarment of starched ruffles, the turn-of-the-century's version of the Miracle Bra; it ends in scallops just above the toes of her own white slippers. Capped with a spray of flowers, the veil falls in layers to her hem, and her enormous bouquet trails ribbons and roses to the floor. "Arrayed for the Bridal" comes to mind, virgins to the sacrifice; it is not so much a dress as a costume. She is not especially pretty. The maid of honor is actually homely with her weak, runkled-up chin; the best man looks a little bug-eyed. Only my grandfather appears handsome, as perhaps befits a raffish young man with a bad temper and no money. In his narrow face, sharp nose, and thick wave of hair, I see more of Eleanor when she was young than the grandfather I recall, a fat, bald old man wearing bifocals and chomping on a big, wet brown cigar.

I cannot date the only photograph of my grandmother alone, for the print I have is a grainy copy blown up on glossy black and white paper. As always, her hair is snagged into a bun that makes her look much older than she lived to be. She is seated on a park bench, one arm resting on the back, her face turned from the camera, her eyes cast down. All but one of the rest are family snapshots so small and blurred they yield no impression. In that one, a sepia-toned portrait that would have been made in 1914, she and my grandfather sit in a parlor with lace curtains at the window and a heavy lace doily on a table topped with a china pitcher. Wearing a long dark skirt and white blouse, she rests one of her boots on a leather footstool and gazes frankly at the camera. Between them on the wood-framed settee, Centa sports the gigantic hairbow that appears in all her childhood pictures, as if an antidote to her limp hair, though at two, round-eyed and chubby, sitting at attention in her dark stockings and little high-buttoned boots, she is too adorable to need the adornment. Eleanor is a bundle of christening clothes in my grandmother's lap. Though in the next picture, occasioned by another christening from the look of Bud's gown, my grandfather has begun to broaden and bald, here he still looks young and handsome. There is something touching in this picture, perhaps the knowledge that he is so soon to age, perhaps the way Centa's small hand rests on his knee, or the pride in the young family that would have summoned the professional photographer to their house, or maybe it is the fact of the two small children and two adults, as if the photographer caught them at the precise moment when their lives seemed to find perfect balance.

But even this photograph fails to bring my grandmother to life. I have invented a hundred characters for fiction, but I cannot give my grandmother breath. I can't get past the paragon of my mother's longing.

When my mother was nearing seventy and beginning to think about her own death, she determined to find her mother's grave. Eleanor knew the name of the cemetery but refused to take her. "Oh, what do you want to see that for?" I can hear her say. She was driving my mother to the airport when she suddenly relented. From the caretaker at St. Marcus they got a map to the unmarked plots. It was my mother's idea to buy a stone. I suppose she told Eleanor because Eleanor lived in St. Louis and could handle the details. She told Ruth because Ruth was her sister. And so of course Ruth and Eleanor chipped in, though Eleanor couldn't see the point and wasn't willing to pay for more than a stake and bronze marker. So they quarreled and Eleanor won.

"I wanted a stone," my mother still says. "I would have paid for it myself." But together they marked their mother's grave, the same grave that has marked my mother's whole life.

A GRAND CANYON

———

MY MOTHER SAID she always wanted to see the Grand Canyon. Actually what she said was "I always wanted to see the Grand Canyon, but I guess I'll never get there." Then the guess fell silent, the comma disappeared, she was sure she'd never get there, and the space between the two clauses grew so short the thought was one, desire and disappointment a single breath. She wasn't going to see the Grand Canyon before she died, and to her it must have seemed a melancholy measure of her life. It did not bother her that she had never seen the Pyramids or Paris; she couldn't understand why anyone would want to travel abroad "when there are so many wonderful things

to see in this country." And for a while after her retirement
she did see a little bit of the US—on a senior tour bus she
went to Nashville, New Orleans, and Niagara Falls, sharing a
room with a widowed acquaintance who lived too many miles
away for any other social congress, but then her acquaintance
moved to Arizona, the tours got too expensive, and she never
did get west. Once, she told me, they were planning to go,
they being my parents, but my father's brother, John, told my
dad he wouldn't like it, and that was that; they went fishing in
Wisconsin. We always went fishing in Wisconsin.

Whether *they* included *we*, my brother and me, or not, I
don't know. Though I recall no such plans, the season between
our departure from home and their divorce was brief, and my
parents were not the kind of people who traveled without children. It's possible that the plans were only my mother's wishful
thinking, but in either case it wouldn't have mattered to me—I
loved the Wisconsin trips, on which I was free to tromp about
the woods, to swim, and best of all when my father got back
from fishing to take the boat. But my mother hated them;
she hated staying in the cabins at the fishing camps, hated
the bathrooms up the hill, and more than that she hated fish.
Yet on those few occasions when she must have insisted on
another destination, my father's Ford invariably developed car
trouble. "Did you hear that noise?" he would wail, and there
was nothing to be done but turn around and drive straight
home, where the suspicious rattle, squeak, or chuff that none
of us could hear always turned out to have been a false alarm.
We went to the Lake of the Ozarks and stayed a single night.
We drove to Albany, taking three days to cross Pennsylvania
on Route 6 because my father didn't want to pay the turn-
pike tolls, but when we got to New York we didn't even spend
the night, never mind that my mother hadn't seen the sister
who lived there since she was a child. Missouri was where

my mother had been born; she had family there too, though I don't recall stopping in St. Louis to visit. On the other hand Wisconsin was where my father's family lived, and on our way to and from the northern lakes we always stayed with John in Menomonee Falls and at the farm outside Eden with his sister, Marie. My mother couldn't stand John, and though she had no quarrel with Marie, she resented the farm, where breakfast, lunch, and dinner for ten meant she never got out of the kitchen. Yet after her divorce she nurtured a conviction that if hadn't been for that, hadn't been for the divorce, she and my father would have spent a happy retirement traveling together.

"All the things we could have seen, think how good we would have had it," she lamented, and when I reminded her that he had never wanted to go anywhere she wanted and that wherever they did go all they did was fight, she would say, "Even so." I think she fixed on the Grand Canyon because it was big enough to hold everything that had failed her.

She was seventy-nine years old when I decided to take her. After all, seeing the Grand Canyon isn't that much to want out of life. I had seen it myself, for my husband's mother too had always wanted to visit the Grand Canyon, and in the summer of 1978 she and my father-in-law brought us along. Besides, I had traveled with my mother before—by her late seventies she no longer drove, and when she came to visit I liked to treat her to an overnight or weekend trip. But the truth is I didn't really *decide* to take her to the Grand Canyon. One night when she began "I always wanted…," I snapped, "I'll take you," because I never wanted to hear the rest of that sentence again.

It is probably needless to mention that my husband chose not to go with us, though it wasn't just the thought of eleven days in a car with his mother-in-law that kept him home. Michael had been there and done that. He has a pathological fear of heights, and one look over the edge nineteen years before had been more than enough grandeur for him. But it was unthinkable that I leave our fourteen-year-old son behind. He had never seen the Canyon. He was eager to go, and we loved traveling together, for we shared a love of nature and a passion for North Carolina's Outer Banks and Blue Ridge Mountains. He knew what to expect; he had traveled with his grandmother before. One of his first memories is chasing seagulls on the lawn in front of Chicago's Museum of Science and Industry while my mother and I sat eating our picnic lunch; he was two. At five he chewed the neck of his Superman T-shirt into a wet rag as he trailed us through Asheville's Biltmore House; at six we rewarded him for enduring the endless tromp through Charleston's historic houses with a ferry to Fort Sumter and a search for lizards at Middleton Plantation; at ten he helped my mother feed the pigeons along the Cape Fear River while we waited for the water taxi to visit the battleship USS North Carolina. At night in the motels my mother took one bed, I took the other, and he spread his sleeping bag beside me on the floor. We played poker for matchsticks, and every hand he had to tell her which cards trumped the others. She never won, and each time she presented a pair she called a full house, he and I laughed at her together. "That's a halfway house, Mom," I said.

I made an agreement with my mother. Though I was finishing a novel, I had another project in the works, a series of miniature American landscapes titled *Because the Land Is Big and Art Is Small*, which was to include two images from every state in Polaroid transfer. I would make all of the arrangements and pay for the trip but wanted to go off by myself sometimes at dawn and dusk to photograph.

"That's fine," she said on the phone, the same way she always says, "Well, I'd better let you go," adding without pause, "Oh, by the way, did I tell you?..." It takes at least three or four

better-let-you-go's for the words to take effect. I was glad that
Max would be along to distract her.

And so on the afternoon of June 18, 1997, Max and I sat
in the Albuquerque airport chatting about our plans while
we waited for my mother's delayed flight from Chicago. He
had a list: he wanted to see a roadrunner, a jack rabbit, a Gila
monster, some Western hummingbirds, and a coyote. I was
looking forward to the Painted Desert, for its ragged, barren
silver-striped hills had seemed almost lunar when Michael's
father drove us through nineteen years before; I felt as if I'd
gone to another planet instead of another part of the country.
But I also wanted to see something I hadn't seen before, and
so we were driving on from the Grand Canyon to Monument
Valley and Canyon de Chelly. I'd already booked Jeep tours of
both as well as a flight over the Grand Canyon.

When I look at the snapshots from those two Southwestern
trips now, the difference between them is apparent at a glance.
Standing between his grandfather and me at the edge of the
Acoma Sky City in the summer of 1978, my eleven-year-
old stepson, Al, just reaches my shoulder. Now in his early
forties, he is perhaps five feet ten, whereas Max stands six
feet eight and wears size 16 extra wide shoes. Examining the
pictures, I try to guess how tall Max was at fourteen. Six feet
five perhaps? At the Grand Canyon guardrail he towers over
me; beside his grandmother, whom osteoporosis had already
shrunk to just over five feet, he looks as if he is posing for
Diane Arbus. His face is scarcely older than Al's—he has a
boy's clearness of eye and smoothness of cheek, a boy's eager,
open expression—but his body has outgrown it.

When my mother arrived, we stuffed our luggage into the
trunk of a dark green Camry; my camera bags and tripod went
on the backseat beside Max. He and my mother began to
squabble over legroom before we left the rental lot. He wanted

her to move her seat forward; she complained her knees were scrunched against the dashboard; when she moved it back he complained that his were in his face. As I drove to our motel in Grants, the elaborate sounds of limbs being tugged, wrenched, and squeezed, exasperated sighs, and bombastic grunts chopped at the silence. My mother's taste in music runs to Grand Ole Opry, but the country station I found sounded too much like rock to her, and unable to find another, I'd turned the radio off. I had bought Max a bag of books and a Walkman for the trip, but he'd forgotten his stash of tapes and had only the tape left in the deck, R.E.M.'s *Document*. He sat in the backseat with his earphones while my mother filled him in on what life had taught her.

"Well, I'll tell you," she began. "Huh?" he asked, pointedly pulling his earphones out each time she twisted to jab his knee or lean across the headrest. "You know, you're a lucky boy, you don't know what a lucky boy you are," she said and began to count his blessings for him as he jammed the phones back in. As he recalls the trip, he listened to R.E.M. a lot.

At Grants, I took a snapshot of them together in the Jacuzzi, then went off to shoot some dusky landscapes at a pond behind the motel. Some of the images of that lonely blue-lit land I made that night and at dawn are among my favorites from the trip, not the landmark landscapes listed on our itinerary, but the unexpected, the surprise. Earlier, as we walked the edge of the pond together, Max had spotted a jack rabbit— only a few hours into the trip he could check the rabbit off his list. It, the crystalline light, and stark beauty of the land seemed to bode well. In the morning Max enjoyed talking to the young guides who drove us up to the Acoma pueblo, "my Native American friends," he called them. My mother was fascinated by an elderly woman so wrinkled her skin seemed fissured, parched as the desert mud, and though I recognized her face from all the Acoma fliers, I happily paid two dollars to take her picture because my mother was so delighted by my rare good luck. From the edge of the mesa we looked out over the desert, my mother scanning the horizon as if she might glimpse the Grand Canyon from there, though we were not scheduled to reach it for another two days.

Back in the car, my mother and Max still haggling over legroom, we passed a scrawny dog. "Oh, look at that poor dog," my mother said and leaned over the seat to poke at Max. "You know these Indians can't afford to feed their dogs like we can. They don't have electricity or running water. You take those things for granted, but when I was a kid we had to leave our door open to get some light from the hall, it was the Depression, we couldn't pay the light bill." He snatched his earphones. "I hate it when Grandma makes those racist comments," he said to me when we stopped.

Though I had hoped to photograph sunset at the Painted Desert, the park closed at seven, and after stopping at a single overlook we drove on to our motel in Holbrook, twenty-four miles beyond. But my mother must have felt she'd already seen it, for when we returned the next morning she scarcely glanced at the sage-spotted, pink and silver striped hills before seating herself on the wall at the overlook with her back to the view and pulling a wallet full of coupons from her purse. "Here. I brought these for you. Do you use Shout? If you buy two you get fifty cents off." "Mom!" I said. "What about Mister Clean? You know if there's anything in here you don't want you can just give it to somebody else." Max was poking around some loose stones at the end of the wall, eyes out for a roadrunner, a golden spray of Prince's plume waving behind him. According to Edward Abbey, the flower indicates poison soil; you can read the land if you know how to look. "Mom! Would you put the coupons away? You're at the Painted Desert. You've never seen it before." "Yes, I know," she murmured, "you're so sweet to take me. Now what about cereal? What kind does Michael like?" Yet she must have put them away, for in the snapshots she sits on the stone wall with her arm around me; we are both wearing sunglasses and khaki shorts, her T-shirt purple, mine green. In another I sit with my leg thrown jauntily over Max's knee, our arms clasped around each other in defiance of my former photo instructor's rule—no hands coming out of nowhere on the shoulders, he cautioned. But we don't look cautioned; we look happy, so happy I think of the children's song:

If you're happy and you know it clap your hands,
If you're happy and you know it clap your hands,
If you're happy and you know it then your face will surely show it,
If you're happy and you know it clap your hands.

How different his expression is in the pictures taken on our deck on his father's birthday two months later. At the edge of the Painted Desert, he is smiling, he has new Native American friends, he's already seen a jack rabbit and is hoping for a roadrunner. On the deck he is sullen and resentful, his face closed off not only to the camera but to us; he has just begun high school, and perhaps he is already skipping, perhaps the first twenty dollar bill has already disappeared from my wallet. His eyes look hostile; I can't tell whether they're unfocused or defiant, only that there is something wrong with them; they're half-lidded. I look at the pictures now and wonder if he's stoned.

But in June he is still my pal, and when we reach Blue Mesa we walk the trail together through the bare hills of blue and gray bentonite clay while my mother waits in the car, just as Michael's parents waited while Michael, Al, and I walked it all those years before, though perhaps because I've seen it before

the loop seems shorter, less magical, the bowl it descends
into smaller, we're not really walking together, he's exploring,
he's examining the spills of petrified logs, I'm taking pictures
and worrying about my mother alone in the car. Yet I needn't
worry. In the last snapshot from Blue Mesa, on the blacktop
of the parking lot just beyond the shadow of the open car door
there is a Chihuahuan raven clutching a big white crumb in its
bill. "He was looking for a handout," my mother says joyfully,
shaking the last particles from a bag of cookies. She loves
animals. If you take her to the ocean she will feed the seagulls
and never see the waves. Max and I should have lingered on
the trail—why didn't we? My mother is fine and he is so soon
to retreat from me—but the shadow is long, it's late, we're tired
and hungry, it's time to move on.

At Walnut Canyon National Monument the next morning
my mother decides to walk the Island Trail with us, not quite a
mile but strenuous according to my guidebook, a steep descent
of 185 feet on a series of steps that will have to be climbed
to get back out, far more demanding than the moderate Blue
Mesa. But it's the only way to see the Sinagua ruins, though by
the time we are eating lunch at a Taco Bell outside of Flagstaff
my mother is clearly more impressed with her stamina than
with the ruins. No one goes to the Southwest to eat at Taco
Bell, of course—Max and I crave real Mexican food, but the
only Mexican food my mother likes are the tacos at Taco Bell.
No matter. My son and my mother are still squabbling over
the arrangement of the car seats, he's begun to roll his eyes and
scowl when she tells him how poor the Indians are and what
a lucky boy he is, but he is a lucky boy, he's seen a jack rabbit
and a roadrunner, he's on his way to the Grand Canyon, we're
on our way, my mother's going to get there in her lifetime, she's
almost there.

—

IT IS LATE AFTERNOON when we drive past our motel to
Mather Point so that my mother can stand at the rail staring into its terraced vastness. Though we all know what the
Canyon looks like from pictures, the actual sight of it still
staggers, for we can experience its stunning scale, the unimag-
inable sublime, only at the edge; only here can we feel what
Edward Abbey calls "the space and light and clarity and
piercing strangeness." Yet we will not really experience the
Canyon; we will not hike to the bottom, we will not descend
into the inner gorge, we will not see Havasu Falls or raft the
river, the two hundred eighty miles of the Colorado that have
carved it; we will not listen to the wind whistle through its
gorges or hear our voices returned to us as echoes by its walls,
we will not know its wildness, we will not know its seasons, we
will not stand on the North Rim, we will only cruise the East
and West Rim Drives, which travel the smallest fraction of the
South Rim, stopping at all the overlooks to behold their post
card views. At Grandview Point I will persuade my mother
to take just a few steps down the trail so that she can say she's
been inside it. At Grand Canyon Village Max and I will leave
her in one of the gift shops and hike half an hour or so down
the Bright Angel Trail, far enough to see the rim rise above
us, to watch a small shimmer of the pastel distance transform
itself into the harder, plainer gray palette of the nearby. We're
reluctant to turn back, but we are after all industrial tourists,
as Abbey calls us. Although my mother was hardly "born on
wheels and suckled on gasoline," for her to see the Canyon it
is necessary that there be scenic vistas, a paved road to reach
them, and parking places when we get there. In fact, the
handicapped permit that came with a knee injury that troubled me for years will not merely come in handy, it is essential
at Mather Point. Imagine spending all that money and traveling all that way and never getting even a glimpse because

you cannot find a space to park. No, we will not really *see* the Canyon, just as I did not really see it on my previous trip. But that's okay, because my mother doesn't really want to *see* it; she simply wants a look. Like the tourists Abbey scorns, she can check it off her list, but there is an important difference between her list and theirs. On hers this is the only item.

And even a look is impressive. Though it is true, as John Wesley Powell observed more than a century before, that "you cannot see the Grand Canyon in one view as if it were a changeless spectacle from which a curtain might be lifted...to see it you have to toil from month to month through its labyrinths," the spectacle is nevertheless quite a spectacle. And even it yields something of the Canyon's grand contradiction, the great dilemma of definition, for it is both presence and absence, both the rock that is there, the rock that we see, the intricate tiers upon tiers and stupefying weight, and the rock that we don't see, not the rock that is behind the next cliff or temple, but the rock that isn't there, the grinding nothingness of the rock that's been eaten away. If we cannot hear its grand stillness, surrounded as we are by the constant clamor of other vacationers, if we cannot hear the swoop of space, in the apprehension of the endlessness of its chasms we can see that such stillness has a shape. Familiarity may prevent us from perceiving it as early explorers did, as a horror, a monstrosity, a vision of hell, but to look straight down is still to experience some measure of its terror. And though the crowded overlook creates something of the atmosphere of a theme park, the Canyon itself is magnificently indifferent to the gate. It is the sight of so much indifference that awes—what Diane Ackerman calls "the absolute, intractable 'other' that human beings face from birth to death," the "steep persuasion of something devastatingly fixed." Yet it is not fixed at all. It appears to be eternal but is a record of change, the sedimentary detritus of one geological epoch heaped upon another, limestone atop sandstone atop shale atop mudstone atop siltstone atop still other sandstones, limestones, shales, and siltstones, atop schists, gneisses, granite dikes and sills, a map of time as well as space, a memory of the blue ocean's repeated advance and retreat, a dance whose steps are so slow we see only the massive ankle rooted to the floor. From where we stand on the relatively young Kaibab limestone of the Coconino Plateau, it is more than ten miles across, yet some of its gorges are so narrow sunlight scarcely penetrates at noon. It is at once the baroque view of the abyss we take in from the top and a steep precipice up from the bottom, the play of light and all its colors and the shadowed darkness of its crevices; it is turrets and buttes, a Zoroaster Temple, Cheops Pyramid, and Tower of Ra; it is also a hanging garden, a wisp of wildflower, a black widow spider, the droppings of a mouse. On the short hike that Max and I take down the Bright Angel Trail we will see a goat, not a mountain goat, but a dingy gray domestic billy, grazing near the trail. Where did he come from? we will say, more startled than if we had come upon a rattlesnake, an elk, a mountain lion. The contradictions it contains will not balance in our heads. We know it as an intimation of a whole or in some intimate part; it is like the vision of the earth from its midst and from the window of the plane. Each is true; yet both exclude the other.

No, we will not see the Canyon—likely I will never *see* it as Powell would have me do—but I have done this much. My mother stands at Mather Point, staring off at Vishnu Temple and Wotan's Throne. There are no coupons in her hand now. The view is priceless.

Tomorrow we will drive to Desert View and take in the Canyon's shallower eastern edge; we will see the Colorado River, hidden a mile below us here, a ribbon the deep teal-green of quarry water tied into a frothy knot around the brown delta where the Colorado and brighter turquoise Little Colorado join. We will walk among the Tusayan Ruins and in the golden light of late afternoon crisscross the Canyon by air, my mother's face pressed to the glass. The day after that we will visit the museum at Yavapai Point and admire the rugs and Kachina dolls at the Hopi House in Grand Canyon Village. In the afternoon we will watch the mules come up from the Bright Angel Trail. They look tired, my mother says. She is tired but happy.

That night she will get sick, very sick.

At dinner she insists upon ordering Mexican though I have picked a restaurant that offers other choices. "But you don't like Mexican food," I protest. "How do I know unless I try it?" she responds. She's adamant, why I'm not sure; it's got ground beef she says, she likes ground beef. Afterwards, while Max and I are at Yavapai Point to photograph the sunset, she begins to vomit. We know it as soon as we open the door, before she says, almost curiously, as if she can't quite comprehend, "I threw up." The room reeks of something that is not an ordinary case of indigestion. She's worried that it's a virus that Max and I will catch too, and though I don't tell her so I worry the same thing. We have reservations at Monument Valley and Canyon de Chelly, days until our flights. She's much too sick to travel; yet we cannot stay here. Rooms are all booked up; even months ago I didn't get my first choice of motels.

All night my mother vomits.

When I take her to the small Grand Canyon Clinic the next morning, we pass rooms where exhausted hikers lie on cots with their boots beside them. My mother's doctor, a young, handsome Navajo, decides to keep her on an IV for the morning. He cannot say whether she has food poisoning or a virus, but sees no reason why we shouldn't go on to Kayenta and promises that by afternoon my mother will be ready for the drive; indeed, when Max and I return after lunch, my mother claps on her white cotton bucket hat. "I'm a tough old broad," she tells the doctor, but in the car she is lifeless, and as we leave the national park I worry where we will find the next bathroom.

There is none at the Little Colorado River Gorge, only a rickety ramada with a few pieces of pottery for sale. At a tourist stop in Cameron she complains the washroom is filthy, and though I'm sorry I have nothing better to offer.

"Well, Mom," I say, "any port in a storm." At Kayenta we leave her at the Holiday Inn to sleep while Max and I drive to Monument Valley. I am concerned about the distance—the tribal park is more than twenty miles from the motel; yet there is really nothing we can do for her but supply Gatorade and let her sleep.

In the morning we take the Jeep tour without her. Our guide is a young Navajo who plays a wooden flute when we stop at the various rock monuments for pictures; he looks scarcely older than Max, who sits beside him in the front seat, grateful for a teenager to talk to. In the gift shop I buy tapes, and the a capella voice of the flute haunts the barren landscape as we drive back to Kayenta, where my mother seems a little stronger, weak but alert enough to begin fussing at Max again as we drive on to Chinle. She wants to put her seat back and recline, and grumpily Max tries to rearrange his legs in the cramped back seat. It tickles her to think she had a Navajo doctor—her Indian medicine man, she calls him.

"Some of these Indians are darn good-looking people," she says as Max fumes. "I wonder if he went to a regular medical school or if they have a special one on the reservation. He seemed just like a regular doctor."

"That's it," Max snaps when we stop. "I'm not riding one more mile with this racist." I try to explain that she doesn't mean it, that any white woman of her generation might say the same things, but my mother's foibles no longer amuse him, he's angry, and so I have to say, "That racist is your grandmother, so shut it and get back in the car."

In Chinle I get her a popsicle and more Gatorade, then take Max to dinner at the A&W, where a drunk begins to pester me for money in the parking lot. He smells like turpentine, and I wonder if Max notices that he's Navajo, a stereotype, the drunk Indian, and am glad my mother is not here to point it out. "Leave us alone," I say, but he follows us inside. He is still demanding money, standing over our table after we order, pulling at my sleeve, though no one else in the restaurant appears to notice. "Look," I say, "I've asked you politely, and if you don't go away right now, I'm going to have to ask my son to deal with you. Stand up, Max." Startled, Max slides from the booth. The drunk stares up at him as if seeing him for the first time, then takes off without a word. "I'm sorry I put you on the spot," I say to Max, but both of us are laughing. He's delighted. "Did you see the look on his face?" he asks.

I buy him a root beer float. "It's too bad your grandmother's sick," I say, though I am happy to have this moment, just the two of us. "She loves these. She always called them black cows."

"That's weird," he says.

In the morning we leave her to sleep in while we take the Jeep tour, traveling into the recesses of Canyon de Chelly, here a verdant terrarium enclosed by pink sandstone walls, there a desert wash of red sand. Our guide is considerably older than the boy at Monument Valley, and he talks to me instead of Max. He has a spiel, and he means to educate us about the Navajo, the ways of the Navajo, the superiority of the Navajo. He wants us to know that we are on Navajo land; if we weren't his guests we would not be allowed inside the canyon. I know this from my guidebook, but he tells me again, and I do not point out that it's a favor for which we are paying very well.

The Anasazi were not the ancestors of the Navajo—in the Navajo language the name means "ancient enemy," he says in a tone that still bears a grudge, though the Anasazi cliff houses and petroglyphs are featured highlights of the tour and his real grudge is not against the Anasazi but us. Later, in the golden light of evening while I photograph a pinyon pine rooted in the russet rock at Junction Overlook, Max strikes up a conversation with a Navajo family selling wares. I buy strings of ghost beads; he selects a sandstone sun. All the way back to the motel he enthuses about the opportunity to get to know some Native Americans, and I haven't the heart to tell him that he doesn't really know them.

On our last morning in Chinle, we take my mother on our drive along the Canyon's North Rim, but she stares at a Navajo hogan and the cows grazing in its grassy depths without interest. "I'm sick," she says. I'm disappointed, but at least I'm no longer worried; she's not nearly as sick as she was. On our way to Albuquerque I order her some roast chicken at a KFC, the blandest option in Window Rock, but she complains it's greasy. What she wants is chicken soup, which I'm pleased to find that night at our motel in Albuquerque, but the broth hasn't been degreased, and she doesn't like that either. Though I can be annoyed with her in restaurants, where she often complains about the food but will not send it back even when the server invites her to, I am not at all annoyed with her now I'm just glad she's well enough to taste it. In the evening she sits out by the pool while Max swims and spies a broad-tailed hummingbird for him. He has missed the Gila monster and the coyote, but three out of five's not bad, and he seems to know it. In the morning he sleeps in while she and I visit the eighteenth century church of San Felipe de Neri. Greasy or not, the soup seems to have helped her. In the afternoon we return the dusty Camry to the rental lot and take the shuttle to the airport. My mother eats half a sandwich in the restaurant, and we see her to her gate. "Bye, Grandma," Max says with a hug. "I love you." *We got through it,* I think. *Been there and done that.*

———

NEVER AGAIN IS THE MORAL when I tell the story of our trip. *Never take a seventy-nine-year-old woman and fourteen-year-old boy to the Grand Canyon.* In that version the canyon is a metaphor for the generation gap between them, and the punch line belongs to me. *That racist is your grandmother. So shut it and get back in the car.* It's a version timed for laughs, because of the way I tell it the journey's over. What I never tell is the journey that's coming, the one I couldn't imagine as Max and I stood watching my mother disappear down the Jetway, even though, unknown to me, it had already begun. I doubt even Max knew then what a wilderness lay waiting exploration inside him. Who could have imagined how we would have to toil through its labyrinths, months stretching into years?

Over the rest of that summer my mother will slowly regain her strength while I finish drafting the novel I left open on my desk. In the meantime Max will go to the swimming pool, the same pool where he once wore baby water wings, and meet up with a girl much too precocious for her age. Abruptly he will drop all his friends to take up with hers. He will grow surly and distant, his expression will harden, the boy's clearness of eye and eager openness will disappear. In the fall he will enter high school, where he will be suspended again and again, he will steal money from me to buy drugs and deny it, he will lie to his therapist, he will hang out with heroin addicts, he will visit a pedophile who will later be murdered in prison, and when we ground him he will run away.

"I'm so worried about you I can't even be angry," I will say.

He will say, "I feel like something broken that can't be fixed."

I don't tell that part of the story, the heartbreaking canyon
that will open between us, because in that part of the story
the generation gap isn't between my mother and my son but
between my son and me. One day the love affair ends for the
child, though it never does for parent.

When my parents divorced my mother did some redecorating. She bought a maple breakfast suite she'd always wanted,
refinished her kitchen cupboards, laid a new floor, hung wall-
paper, installed interior shutters, tiled a backsplash, bought a
new stove and refrigerator in harvest gold. When she finished
one room she moved on to another. It's not that unusual a
thing to do following a divorce; yet she did it, by her account,
not just because she didn't care for the furnishings my father
had picked out or because she didn't want those reminders, but
because she wanted me to know her.

What I leave out of the story I tell about our trip is the
absurdity of that desire to be known by our children or even to
know them. We were lucky, for the story I don't tell ends much
the same as the one I do. We got through it. The most insen-
sitive and cavalier of our friends was right. Max got over it;
whatever had broken was repaired. But the son who came back
to us is not the boy who left. As children always do, he grew
up and became someone else, a young man I love more than
anything on earth even though I will never know him in the
way I once thought I knew the boy.

Yet in another way the story doesn't end, for we live as the
Canyon does, changing so slowly we scarcely notice, but even
in the stillest of moments in flux. My mother is ninety now,
and I am aware of time in a way I have not been before. The
rooms she took such pride in redecorating have frayed; with
a wave of her hand she says, "Having everything match, I'm
beyond that now." She could not think of negotiating the steps
into Walnut Canyon; I cannot imagine holding her hand to

coax her down the fewest feet of Grandview Trail. I have to hold her arm to guide her down the three stairs of my front porch, and even so she falls. And every time we talk she asks me again my son's address. It's no longer just straights and flushes she forgets.

Max has been gone for more than seven years, he's finished college, and his friends, his housemates, and his dog are what his family once was, the thread that runs through the daily fabric of his life. And even still I miss him so acutely that the sight of a mother holding her little boy up to the sink in a ladies room is enough to make me weep. I miss the shared jokes and observations; I miss his conversation. Yet when he calls, I have come to cherish the stillness between us, those moments of silence when neither of us can think what else to say and yet we hold on, balanced over the gorge of years and miles between us by the will and need to connect, which is the connection itself, more enduring than knowledge, poised on nothing but the air of memory and love, as solid as the rock that once was there, supported, suspended, sustained.

MUD PIES

—-—

We were sitting on the curb with our legs sprawled in the
gutter of the dead-end of Sixty-third Place off Drexel, making
mud pies. It's hard to imagine there could have been enough
mud, just the dust that settled at the edges of the street, but
we were city girls, we made do. This was Chicago, late 1940s,
South Side. I don't remember now if my friend was black or
white, though I think that she was black; she may have been the
new landlord's daughter. "Who *is* that man?" I'm told I asked
the first time I saw him in the building where we lived in a
third-floor one-bedroom walk-up with linoleum rugs and a bay
window in the living room where I slept, a giant step up from

the single room with a shared kitchen and a landlady who didn't allow children that we occupied when I was born. He may have been the first black man I ever saw, though I doubt it. You can't rely on me: I was three or four years old. All I remember is the two of us sitting with our legs sprawled in the gutter, making mud pies. That and the woman screaming.

Until she screams this memory has no soundtrack. We were two little girls seated on the curb with our feet, in the round-toed perforated red leather shoes my mother called barefoot sandals, stuck out in the street. Surely we whispered and giggled, our faces bent close together, but as the big shiny black car backed up to park we raised our heads, watching with a kind of spellbound curiosity that mutes and stalls the moving world. Whether it was the sight of the fancy car that transfixed us, a magnetic sense of what would happen, or just the notion that this was our space, *we-were-here-first*, I can't say, only that we sat and watched. Perhaps there was a crunching sound like gravel, surely the girl screamed, though I don't recall her cry, only the hysterical shrieking of the woman. There were two of them, a man and a woman, I'm sure that they were white, and though I've said that she was driving, it may have been him. They lifted my playmate into a child's red wagon, where she sat with her legs straight out in front of her, her eyes round and solemn as they pulled her into the dark first-floor hall of the apartment house. The landlord may have been a doctor, or perhaps the doctor who was summoned was black. I remember the round, shiny black dome of his head and the dull, crinkled black leather of his valise, and then the hall door shutting in my face.

I don't recall seeing the girl again, though perhaps the car only grazed her; she may not have been badly hurt. To children things just happen, and that's the end of it. Their questions command no answers; they are powerless to ask. In any case, our neighborhood, Woodlawn, was in transition. "You have to get out," the white shopkeepers along Sixty-third Street urged my mother in buzzing whispers. She had her brother drive us to Hammond, Indiana, where she bought a tiny house in a tract so new the cement stoops and half-built walls still jutted from the mud, all that mud, yard after yard of it spread out like a sea, a suburban sanctuary in the making where little white girls wouldn't have to make their pies in the street. It's possible I never saw my playmate again simply because we moved away.

It was the accident that stamped this into memory, of course. So many early memories, and not just mine, are of unpleasant things, for those are the events that stand out from the rest, that make a lasting impression. Yet the memories themselves do not feel unpleasant, and this is not a traumatic one for me. If there was blood, I don't recall it; nor does the recollection evoke survivor's panic, that rush of thought that articulates itself as a current through the body, a trilled whisper through the nerves, *that victim could have been me.* Rather, this memory seems almost pleasant, pleasant because the act of reclaiming anything so dimly distant is sweet. It is as if I possess a photograph of myself sitting on a curb in Chicago, a little girl in a thin cotton pinafore making mud pies, a photograph unlike any of the many pictures of my childhood in my mother's album, for it's one I took myself. In it I am not my mother's child but myself, my own invention. I am not a child in a world of adults, but a child in the world of children. And the Chicago that photograph lays claim to is not my mother's but my own.

My mother is skeptical. She has no memory of the incident. "You never went outside to play alone," she objects, then corrects herself. "Well, I always tried to keep an eye on you from the third floor. I wouldn't let you play out there like that now, I can tell you." Her voice climbs in a way that seems to call for concurrence, and so I assure her of the obvious: "It's a different world, Mom."

"I took good care of you. I read you two stories every night," she says, warming to her own memory. "And man did you ever fuss if I tried to skip a single word. I think you knew every story by heart, but you wanted me to read them anyway. Do you remember that?" As a matter of fact, I don't. I was too young, and so that narration is hers, just as most of my early childhood belongs to her and my son's belongs to me, which is why he has so little interest in it. But there's no sense quibbling, for I know that she read to me and that her reading helped shape my imagination. And though I don't remember the warm throne of her lap or the cadence of a story in her voice, I do remember the books. My mother was not a literary woman; before the Depression forced her to drop out of school, her favorite subject was math, and the sensibility she brought to the Little Golden Books she chose was shaped by the practical. The surreal nonsense of a Lewis Carroll was not for her. Even today she says of *Alice's Adventures in Wonderland*, "I never cared for that story"; to her *Alice* will always be just a poor investment of the twenty-five cents she scrimped from the grocery fund every other week to finance my reading. *The Poky Little Puppy* and *Busy Timmy*, with their lessons in promptitude, self-sufficiency, and tidiness, were more to her taste.

But one of our favorite books was called *Let's Go Shopping*. I can still see the protagonists, a rosy-cheeked brother and sister with dark curly hair, bent so far forward by anticipation they are nearly horizontal as they race downtown to spend their precious pennies. As I recall, the book was a tour of the city shops and the things that they might buy, but the freedom with which they roamed the downtown streets and stores was far more alluring to me than any merchandise. The faces of the salesclerks never appeared; their parents might as well have been on Mars. We couldn't know, my mother and I, what a perfect little period piece that book would prove, for by the time I went to school and learned to read for myself, book children had all turned blond and moved to the suburbs, where their adventures too seemed to pale under the watchful eyes of their doting and insipid parents. Of course, by then we too had moved from the city to the suburbs.

We never went back, not to the city we had known, the neighborhood streets that we had walked. The Great Migration had claimed Chicago's South Side, its spacious old bay-windowed apartments divided into kitchenettes and then torn down, replaced by the strip of uniformly bleak high-rise projects that would later be torn down themselves, the infamous Robert Taylor Homes. "You can't go back," my parents said with a shudder that implied merely to drive down Drexel Avenue would be more dangerous than attempting to negotiate Niagara Falls in a barrel. By the time I was six the Chicago of the '40s pictured in my mother's album, my other favorite book—the curve of the streetcar tracks disappearing around a corner, the cement balustrades of the Jackson Park promenades, the rocky Sixty-seventh Street beach, Navy Pier and its day-cruise ships with their one-armed bandits, most of all, the light-striped tunnel of darkness beneath the tracks of the Sixty-third Street el—seemed as fabled, as fabulous and lost to me as if it had been another country. Ten years before the Berlin Wall, the South Side of Chicago might as well have drawn an Iron Curtain around it. What imprinted itself deeply on my imagination when I was young was not the uncharted territory of the unexplored but the irreclaimable land of the exile.

I suppose Hammond was a sanctuary of sorts, where no one needed to keep an eye on the children who played outside, for there were plenty of us, the proverbial safe numbers, and nowhere to go beyond the tame streets of our tract. Together we jumped rope, played Mother-May-I, hopscotch, tag, and Red Rover; we roller skated up and down the sidewalks on the metal clamp-on skates that sent the cracks and texture of the pavement jangling up through our skulls, traded baseball cards, dug snow forts, made snowmen. But I was not like my brother, who was an infant when we moved and had no memory of the clattering that was the el or the faint humming of streetcar wires, of the cement alleyways wide as streets or the broad expanse of the Midway Plaisance, where I had gone ice skating with my father, of the Lake Michigan waves breaking into a cool white spray against the rocks, or the way the numbered streets all seemed to stream toward the distant silver-green glade of Jackson Park. Names like Racine, Halsted, Cottage Grove, and Kimbark Avenue had no special resonance for him. Our bland and treeless plain of identical one-story frame houses lay just below 173rd Street, as if Hammond had taken upon itself the task of reminding us the exact number of blocks that separated me from what my mother had convinced me was the very center of the universe, the place where all the numbers in the world came back to zero, the corner of State and Madison. But while one hundred and seventy-three blocks closed me out of the mythical city, they could not take me as far as the country, which we visited whenever we spent the weekend with my father's sister in Wisconsin. There we cousins tore through the woods, skirting the cow patties in the pasture, hopping from hummock to hummock in the marshy field down by the creek as we chased one another in our games of hide and seek. It was awkward playing host when they spent the night with us, for the suburban blocks that encased us suddenly seemed even more monotonous and confined. Where could we have hidden? There were no nearby parks, no playgrounds, no woods, just sidewalk after sidewalk, house after what surely seemed to them featureless house.

For a brief time after we moved to Hammond my mother
liked to visit a friend who still lived in Chicago, somewhere in
the seventies just west of Stony Island in South Shore. How
I liked to walk up that wide avenue glittering with mica to
the dime store where we drank ice cream sodas at the lunch
counter beneath the whirring ceiling fans, the two women
nudging their baby strollers back-and-forth along the worn
hardwood floor. If I was lucky my mother would let me choose
a book of paper dolls, and I pressed the bag tight to the front
of my gingham dress as we left the store, not minding that
we walked southward, with our backs to the magical corner
where Stony Island swept into Jackson Park. Then my mother's
friend too moved to Hammond, to a street that dead-ended
into the steep gravel embankment of the new expressway, and
our visits were bound by the walls of her dark living room and
its persistent smell of fried meat. Years later, when I visited
Harlem for the first time, I was struck by how much more
the breadth of 135th Street and the thriving business district
around 125th and Lenox Avenue resembled the South Side
of Chicago than the rest of Manhattan. I hadn't set foot to the
South Side in fifty years; yet I experienced the same visceral
thrill of coming home as I did when I moved from southern
Indiana to Richmond, Virginia in my twenties and was nearly
overwhelmed with a sense of recognition that felt as if it
welled up through my feet from the pavement into my lungs
and set my heart to race at the mere sight of the five-story
Miller and Rhoads in the then thriving downtown or the brick
row houses on Church Hill and in the Fan with their narrow
gangways and stacked tiers of gray wooden back porches
that I remembered with a sudden clarity that seemed to live
inside my body, a pre-memory of the city that can't be erased
because it's in my blood. I would not pretend that I actively
miss Chicago lest I be accused of sentimentality—I was not

yet five years old when I left—yet I do feel nostalgia, the kind
Pete Hamill speaks of in his book about Lower Manhattan,
Downtown. Sentimentality is about lies, he says, nostalgia
about "real things gone," not so much about what we remember, but itself "an almost fatalistic acceptance of the perma-
nence of loss." The body cannot remember a lie.

Although I identify with exiles, who tend to turn up in my
fiction uninvited, I would feel pretentious to name myself
among them, for anyone who compared my experience to that
of a Russian who fled the Bolsheviks, a Jew who anticipated
the Holocaust and set sail, a Cambodian who escaped the
killing fields, a Montagnard, a Hmong, a Rwandan, or Lost
Boy of Sudan would find mine trivial and wanting. My birth-
right wasn't stolen; it was not an evil force that displaced us.
By nearly all accounts we who left were the villains, guilty of
panic; it won't do to aggrandize my loss or to whine. Years later,
when I was a graduate student for a year in the Blue Ridge
Mountains of southwestern Virginia, I lived in a cottage tacked
on the back of a big lodge in the country that was rented by a
family of aristocratic Cubans who had fled Fidel Castro and
his henchmen. Later that year Papa Gaston as we called him,
for he looked just like the grizzled Ernest Hemingway of later
years, would be called to design the first high-rise hotel in
Cancún, a project he'd intended for Havana when he submit-
ted it as his thesis in architecture at Harvard some twenty-five
years before. I heard the story of their escape from his wife,
Marguerite, when I asked if they would please lock their doors
at night, for the cottage my housemate and I shared opened
into their back hall, and it did us no good to lock our doors if
they did not lock theirs. There is a story as to why we wanted
to lock our doors, but it pales beside hers, which was a harrow-
ing tale, long and difficult to follow as a result of her accent
and lapses into Spanish, and though it seemed a digression

with its tangle of details about a hunting trip, some caves, a firing squad, and private plane, details I never did get straight, what I finally understood was that the story was her answer. She and her husband saw no point. They had lost whatever faith they might once have had that a locked door could keep anyone safe.

Though what displaced us, my parents and me, was not a revolution or a war, we too marched to the drum of history, a demographic shift so extreme in numbers and profound in effect that historians have dubbed it the Great Migration. Its first wave had begun, unknown to my parents, around the time that they were born, when the boll weevil destroyed the cotton crop in the south at roughly the same time the first World War created a demand for industrial goods and a shortage of labor in the north. By the end of World War I fifty thousand African Americans had left the ravaged farms of Dixie for the city that the most influential black publication in the country, *The Chicago Defender*, portrayed as the promised land. By the time the second wave began in the early 1940s, Elijah Muhammad had already moved the headquarters for his Nation of Islam from Detroit to Chicago, and Harlem was no longer the capital of black America. Again there was a war, that impetus for industry, the war my parents remember, and when the mechanical cotton picker went into mass production in 1944, the year of my birth, Chicago, with its railroads and massive meat-packing business, became the most important destination for African Americans heading north. My parents couldn't know the statistics or the reasons, only the effect: over the course of a decade Chicago's black population increased by seventy-seven percent, all concentrated where we lived, on the South Side. More than two thousand African Americans were moving to Chicago every week, and the traditional black ghetto, the neighborhood around the Twelfth Street bus and train stations, could no longer accommodate them. The man who bought our apartment building on Drexel was just one of a growing black middle class looking to escape the overcrowding and deteriorating conditions by moving to the lower-middle-class white neighborhood of Woodlawn. Over the next decade, as the black population continued to increase, that middle class would push farther and farther south, until Chicago's black belt extended all the way to the city limit. There were riots, including one in nearby Park Forest in 1949, the year we would move to Hammond. It's possible my mother feared there would be a riot in Woodlawn, though I didn't know to ask when she was younger, and she wouldn't remember now.

In any case, I doubt my parents ever fully grasped the scope of the migration or its causes. It's hard to see the shape of history from its midst. Perhaps to them too things simply seemed to happen. For them white flight was not a matter of property values; they owned nothing. They were poor people born into World War I; their teen years were shaped by the Depression, their young adulthood and first years of marriage by the ration lines of World War II. My mother spent part of her childhood in an orphanage; my father lived with his grandparents because his mother had TB. They were not of a generation, an experience, or a class whose children were encouraged to believe that they could control their own fate. In fact my father felt that the most important advice he could pass along to his own children was "Don't rock the boat."

My mother used to enjoy reminiscing about how she met my father at the Trianon Ballroom, where they had both gone to hear Lawrence Welk. "Of course all that's gone now," she would say with a shake of her head, as if the Trianon, indeed the whole South Side, had vanished with nothing to take its place. But of course it didn't vanish; it only vanished for us. In college I discovered the blues and fell in love. To think how close I was to the Chicago blues scene and didn't know it, I sometimes lament to my blues–and jazz-loving husband, as if my parents would have permitted their teenaged daughter to hang out in the South Side clubs where Muddy Waters, B.B. King, Little Milton, and Little Walter reigned. *Their* audiences didn't miss Tommy Dorsey or Lawrence Welk. We're the ones who spent our Saturday nights listening to the Lennon Sisters and champagne music on our black and white TV. Even when I was in college, taking the South Shore to meet friends in the Loop, what I knew of the South Side was confined to the view from the train window, the strip of projects that stood like a sixteen-story wall between me and the city my mother's city had become. The train didn't stop until it reached Roosevelt Road and the trio of museums at the foot of the Loop. Type "Chicago neighborhoods" into Google, you won't find Woodlawn in the list you bring up, and though it's a bright yellow block in the neighborhood grid in my Chicago *Flashmaps*, you'll look in vain through the book's pages for a street map, just as most of my maps of Manhattan stop shy of Harlem at Central Park North.

It didn't occur to me that my mother, who had never lived more than a block off Sixty-third Street since she was a tot, also missed the city. It had been her decision to move. In the egocentricity of childhood I'm sure I believed adults didn't care about the aesthetics of living; later, when I was twelve or thirteen, pouting over a new dress we couldn't afford and she pointed out that she wasn't getting a new dress either, I would tell her that she didn't need one, she didn't care, she was old. Now she really is old and by her own account much beyond caring. She sees no irony in the fact that her neighborhood in Hammond is no longer all white, and when I try to talk her into moving—not because the neighborhood has changed, but because I worry about her cleaning gutters and shoveling snow—she says simply, "I'm not going anywhere." The Chicago she returns to again and again is not the fabled, lost place of her independence and youth, but the cold and hungry world of her childhood. The loss of her mother at an early age weighs more heavily each year; the loss of the city cannot compare. And so it is I who revisit those images and fragments—the bars of light striping the faces of the uniformed staff of Merritt's Sixty-third Street Cafeteria as they pose beneath the clattering shadow of the el, the hum of the streetcar wires; the hiss of the tires on the bicycles she and her girlfriends rented to pedal through Jackson Park; the feel of the white gloves and hats and crisp bolero dresses they wore to window-shop the Loop; the scent of a shaggy corsage in a tinted dime store photo that was all my mother would accept from the florist who proposed on their second date because, well, that was a little odd, she says, and besides she was having so much fun on her own; and then the long slow glide up the grand staircase to the Trianon Ballroom, where she would meet my father—all the unencumbered pleasures she would have lost anyway to the responsibilities of marriage and motherhood, for it is indeed a different world, spinning farther every day into a future in which we are all exiled from the domains of our youth by time.

I used to believe that my nostalgia was so intense because I felt I had lost something I never possessed. But the truth is that we do not possess our lives. As true exiles know, we stand too easily to lose them, and in the end we are all just passing through. It is what we remember of the journey that we possess. I own a little girl sitting on a curb in Chicago in the barefoot sandals her mother always made her wear with socks, and in the curious stillness of that moment when she looks up from her mud pie and cocks her head in wait, I know now that what she is waiting for is something to remember.

BLACK WIDOW

———

I HADN'T THOUGHT THEY would be so small. In my imagination they were huge, and why not since my only previous encounter had come in a Nancy Drew book? I no longer remember which one, only that when the crook—a counterfeiter or jewel thief, some sort of greedy schemer—locked the girl detective in a room full of black widow spiders and turned out the light, a shudder slipped down my spine. I could feel them crawling closer, deadly with venom and villainous intent. Never mind that I knew she'd survive, knew even then that there was no real mystery at the heart of the mysteries she solved. Evil in her world was all menace and no force, the evil-doers stupid, and the evil itself easily parsed. But if the villains were petty, the spiders were mythic, black-hearted, potent, larger than life, on a par with tarantulas, piranhas, cobras, and boa constrictors, exotic creatures of unspeakable horror. I was the more terrified for having nothing to fear, living as I did in a brand new ranch house on a treeless street in Hammond, Indiana. Where would a jewel thief or black widow hide? I had never even seen a cockroach.

My mother had. In a Chicago apartment she had fought an army of roaches with J-O Paste spread on slices of raw potato. She laid her weapons out after she deposited me in my crib for the night and took them up before I woke so that I wouldn't eat them. I was young enough to do that, which is to say too young to remember. Except for fragments, my memory begins in the clean new rooms of our first house in Hammond, in the bright cinder block classrooms of the new elementary school, a suburban Eden so banal no snakes were allowed. Outside an occasional daddy-long-legs might run across your arm, but we all know *they* can't hurt you. When I cut through the weedy vacant lot at the corner on my way to school, grasshoppers leapt into my crinolines, pinging against my bare legs and spitting their brown tobacco juice on the stiff white layers, but by year's end the field was gone, and a tidy row of shops stood in its place. In Wisconsin I stepped in a yellow jackets' nest, and the wasps chased me down the beach near our cottage, but that was the wilderness; we *lived* in a world that we could master. When a plague of thirteen-year "locusts" invaded Hammond with their repulsive big black bodies and googly red eyes, I simply refused to go outside. I wasted years dreading their next cyclical return, which proved anticlimactic, for by then I was grown and living downstate in a lush landscape that hid them from view.

Or perhaps by then I was able to take cicadas in stride. My first husband and I had spent the initial year of our marriage in a house skittering with roaches fed on the rich black Midwestern loam. There were rats inside the walls; at night we heard them squealing, and when I called the landlady to complain, it took her several moments to respond. "Well," she said finally, "do you suppose your man could set a trap?" I looked at the man I had just married, a PhD student in literature who had grown up on a country club golf course. "I don't think so," I said, and we called an exterminator, who took up the floorboards beneath our bed, put out his poison, and nailed the boards back. We went away for Thanksgiving, and when we got back there was a bloated dead mouse in the bathtub.

But I never saw a black widow. The spider seemed so sinister it was more apocryphal than real, not so much fictional as *there not here*, like the boa, the piranha, the cobra. Even its name is the stuff of legend, its common name, that is, for its scientific name, *Latrodectus mactans*, means "biting in secret," an accurate description. It is the praying mantis that would more aptly be called "widow," since the female routinely bites off the male's head and begins to consume him even before they're done mating. Of the widow spiders only the southern black eats the male, and that is an exception rather than the rule. She may even feed him if he hangs around after mating, though more often he simply crawls away. He's of no use to her now; she will continue to reproduce without him. Like most male spiders he has little to do, he can't protect their kids, he can't even protect himself, he doesn't bite, he carries no venom. *Her* bite is vicious, and she is especially likely to strike after mating, which leaves her hungry and cross. Her venom is the most deadly of all spiders, a neurotoxin fifteen times more potent than that of the rattlesnake, though she injects such a small amount most human victims recover. Nevertheless she is responsible for nearly all spider bite fatalities in the United States.

Before I went to Arkansas for grad school, the tarantula too seemed a creature of legendary danger. European folklore

once attributed a hysteria called tarantism to its bite, the chief
symptom of which was a mania to dance, hence the Italian
dance called the tarantella, which was supposed to cure tarantism, no doubt on the same theory that gave us the hair of
the dog. In fact the culprit was almost certainly the European
widow spider, cousin of our southern black, and the dance a
kind of seizure, but the tarantula, actually a large, sedentary
wolf spider, got the blame and the name, *Lycosa tarantula,*
from the Italian town of Taranto. Unlike the widow, which
uses its web to trap food, immobilizing the victim by wrap-
ping it in silk, the tarantula is a hunter, chasing down reptiles
and amphibians, even small birds, rearing back to strike with
its fangs, grasping the paralyzed victim with appendages
located between its mouth and legs, grinding it into a ball,
then vomiting the digestive juices that will liquefy it before the
spider sucks it down. Fortunately its venom is not nearly so
toxic to humans, although the barbed hairs it kicks off its back
in defense can be highly irritating to the eyes and nose. Still,
it's not surprising the Italians would vilify the tarantula rather
than the small, unobtrusive widow. Tarantulas *look* dangerous.

For one thing they're huge. In 1954 Hollywood crossbred
our fear of the bomb with our fear of insects to create the sci-fi
film *Them!,* in which radiation from atomic testing produced
a strain of murderous thirty-foot ants that terrorized the
Southwest and begat a whole genre of giant critter horror
flicks, including, of course, one called *Tarantula.* To most fans
these B movies seem more like high camp than horror, but
for serious arachno- and entomophobes they're not funny,
and among Caucasians arachnophobia is one of the most
common phobic disorders, for in the Middle Ages Europeans
believed spiders caused the plagues that swept the continent
and their fear became so culturally ingrained that it is nearly
as hereditary as celiac disease or cystic fibrosis. (According to

Piotr Naskrecki, former Director of the Invertebrate Diversity
Initiative, the seemingly irrational fear of spiders and insects is
a form of "prepared learning" with a scientific basis, since for
millions of years human evolution has favored individuals who
avoided small creatures.) A scene in which crew members were
eaten by giant spiders proved so terrifying in test screenings of
the original *King Kong* it had to be cut. Better to be pursued by
a giant ape than a big spider.

Certainly Miss Muffet would have thought so, for the little
lady of the nursery rhyme was a real girl named Patience
Muffet whose notorious fear of spiders was nurtured by her
stepfather, sixteenth-century English naturalist Thomas Muffet
(or Moufet). Dr. Muffet, who believed spiders prevented gout
among other diseases, was such an enthusiast he kept them as
pets, giving them the run of his house. Poor Patience—to cure
her fevers he rolled spiders in bread crumbs and fed them to
her live; for colds he applied a poultice of their urine and dung
to her eyes. Henry Wadsworth Longfellow's "Evangeline"
offers a variation of Muffet's treatment when his heroine is
told that a spider shut up in a nutshell will cure a fever, though
she fails to save her love from the "pestilence" that befalls him.
It can't be that she didn't have a spider handy, for, "Wherever
you are there is a spider within a meter of you," according to
Adrienne Mason in *The World of the Spider*. Like Miss Muffet,
Evangeline undoubtedly considered the treatment worse than
the disease.

Arkansas is full of spiders, a fact that goes unadvertised in
tour guides and university bulletins. I had no idea tarantulas
inhabited the state until I sat on the edge of a bluff in Devil's
Den State Park one October afternoon and glimpsed a dark,
hairy leg scurrying past my outstretched hand. The append-
age was so big that for a moment I thought my boyfriend
had played a joke and snuck my kitten into the park. A friend

found a tarantula curled like a cat in the corner of her sofa; the next time I saw one it was inside my car. They can't hurt you, Arkansans insisted. Not if you manage to keep from driving off the cliff when one hitches a joy ride.

One evening as I sat reading in my little house in Fayetteville, a black spider half as big as my hand dropped into my lap. I jumped up and screamed, but there was small comfort in its disappearance since I had to go to bed knowing it was loose in the house. Several people I knew, including the man who would become my second husband, had been bitten by the brown recluse. I went around the house on a rampage, wielding a can of Raid, and killed thirty-seven spiders behind a single bookcase. Legs drawn up, brown fiddles on their backs. Were they *all* the dangerous *Loxosceles reclusa*? Rick Vetter of the University of California, Riverside, Department of Entomology says check the map; if you do not live in an area that is supposed to have recluse spiders it is highly unlikely your spider is one. It's clear that he feels people misidentify everything from a daddy-long-legs to a Volkswagen as the brown recluse. Because so many people have mistaken mark-ings on spiders as violins, the fiddle shape is not a reliable indicator for a non-arachnologist, he warns; you need to look at the eye pattern. I confess I did not look my spiders in the eyes. I can't say whether they had six pairs (the recluse) or eight in two rows of four. Mind, the spider is about three-eighths of an inch long; if you want to count eyes you're going to have to come close. Doctors say that if you're bitten you should bring the spider in for positive identification. They also say you're unlikely to know you've been bitten, for more often than not the wound is painless until it begins to fester. When you come down with fever and chills, you might think you have the flu, but the recluse's venom is a necrotoxin; you'll know you've been bitten when the gangrene sets in.

There were mice in the house in Fayetteville too. A previous tenant had put out an off-brand poison, which dropped them in their tracks but failed to dry them up. We'd smell that tell-tale something sweetish, a pink smell I call it, and start hunting. Nancy Drew may have had to contend with a roomful of black widows, but I'm willing to bet *she* never had to pick up a dead mouse. She was never startled by big black water beetles huddling in the sinks of her beach cottage at night. There were no weevils breeding in her pantry, no silverfish caught in the slick at the bottom of her soap dish, no caterpillars tenting in her trees, or moths devouring the frocks in her closet. When she felt her way around an old attic or dank cellar, all she found were clues.

I could claim a rational aversion. Twice since I moved to North Carolina I have been bitten by the brown recluse. I have survived Rocky Mountain spotted tick fever; my husband has been treated for Lyme disease. Our basement is open to a crawl space infested with camelback crickets, huge, hideous, unpredictable leapers that bear no resemblance to Jiminy. One summer we were overtaken by earwigs, slithering out of flowerpots, dropping from the shrubbery, scattering every time I opened the grill; indoors I had to pick them from my hair, their dark pincers wagging as they secreted their rank, oily smell.

Another year carpenter ants, ants as big as boxcars, crawled out of our dishwasher to bite us. Bees nested in the ceiling of our bay window; we could hear them buzzing as we sat down to breakfast. Rats got into the garage, and when Terminix failed to finish them off, my husband bought a pellet gun, and he and our son sat on the deck and shot them. That took care of that, I thought, until a brick fell out of our foundation and a new generation snuck in to file their teeth inside my kitchen cupboards.

But I never saw a black widow. Though we dealt with the
mice, dealt with the rats, dealt with the bees and the ants and
learned to tolerate the crickets and the earwigs, the spider
remained the stuff of girls' detective novels, far too mythic
for an actual appearance. And so imagine my shock when I
reached for a shovel inside the garage shortly after we moved
to the big old house where we still live and tickled something
sticky—there she was in the corner, hanging upside down from
her web, unmistakable, the secret biter, a shiny black bulb with
a sharp clench of legs and the telltale bright red hourglass on
her abdomen. Here not there. Real and so much smaller than
my imagination, the deadly venom cupped inside a body no
more than a quarter inch long. A cobweb spider, she uses a
comb on her fourth leg to spin a web so small and tangled
you might not notice it until you touch it, might not realize
there's a spider inside, out of sorts and ravenous from mating.
You hold the deed, but it's her territory, and the survival of the
species depends upon her. When she strikes, you may feel a
pinprick or nothing at all. You'll know it was a widow when
the abdominal pain hits, so severe you might think it appendi-
citis, when your muscles and the soles of your feet start aching,
when you begin to drool and then your mouth goes dry, when
your eyelids swell and you soak your clothes with sweat, when
your chest locks and you can't breathe and then you understand
without being told that the way her victims die is to suffocate.
If you're over sixty or under ten, you might worry.

My son was not yet two when I found a nest of black widows
beneath the seat of his sandbox. Their egg sacs, I've learned,
can hold as many as a thousand eggs, and there must have been
hundreds of tiny spiderlings ballooning into the sand. I rushed
my baby inside, and we demolished the box. Later I read that
before indoor plumbing was standard widows liked to spin
their silk beneath the outhouse seat; bites on the genitalia of

the male were particularly common. No wonder they seem not merely dangerous but evil. They are so secretive one rarely sees them, but only last week my son called to report that he had found two beneath his windowsills. Though Michael read him nearly all of *Charlotte's Web* the day we brought him home from the hospital as an infant, it did no good: spiders creep him out. His last house was infested with large gray spiders, so big and so numerous he and his housemates stashed pellet guns beside every chair. "They made a mess when you shot them," he reports. "Wolf spiders," I guess; some, he agrees, but others were not; they had smooth yellowish-gray banana-shaped bodies. "Show me," I ask, handing him my field guide—I want to call by name these spiders large enough to draw a bead on from across the room—but he can't find them, though they were as real as the black widow that dropped from her web to the floor when I cleaned beneath the china cabinet this morning.

"Will you walk into my parlor?" said the spider to the fly. Even kings have spiders in their palaces according to the Bible.

How could I have imagined that the world I lived in was safe? Only a year ago a local woman died of a black widow bite, or so a friend reports—she heard about it at a party. Is the story true? According to the internet no one in the United States has died from a black widow bite in more than ten years. There *was* a woman who died of Rocky Mountain spotted tick fever the same month; I read the cause of death in her obituary. Could the stories have been conflated? I can't find a report; the hospital doesn't release information. I can believe whatever I choose.

But it's wearisome to spend your days recoiling from the creatures that surround you. E.B. White didn't. He was so fascinated by the pregnant *Aranea cavatica* who served as the model for Charlotte, he was unwilling to part with her though he had to leave his farm in Maine to return to New York, and so he took her with him, cutting the sac from the underside of his shed roof, and putting spider and sac in a candy box. A few weeks later, he was "pleased to find that Charlotte's daughters were emerging from the air holes in the cover of the box," stringing tiny lines from his comb to his brush to his mirror to his nail scissors. They were very busy and almost invisible, he reported, and they all lived together happily for a couple of weeks until somebody whose duty it was to dust his dresser balked and he "broke up the show." Better to emulate White than his housekeeper, I decided. And so one summer I bought an expensive micro lens and ring flash for my Nikon and went out to the garden to make friends. On the gaillardia I watched a little hover fly with its smooth bee-colored stripes, cellophane wings, and huge, sober fly eyes. Pennsylvania leatherwings were mating on my autumn sedum, which was trembling with checkered beetles and rowdy-colored ailanthus webworm moths. My garden was a circus, leafhoppers in one ring, in the others a purple and orange grapeleaf skeletonizer and harlequin cabbage bug, so brightly colored they might have been wearing motley. Even the carapace of the stink bug was a handsome bright green rimmed with the most delicate band of yellow.

In insects color matters. We loathe the homely brown cockroach while the sight of a green treehopper, a katydid, or even the big emerald-colored June bug delights. Though their blood is poisonous to birds, nearly everyone loves ladybugs, which were associated with the Virgin Mary in the Middle Ages, though you hardly need a holy connection to sense that killing one is bad karma. Garden stores sell them to control aphids, and for centuries children have recited the rhyme inspired by the European practice of burning hop vines after harvest—*Ladybird, ladybird, fly away home/Your house is on fire, your children alone*—for the flightless ladybird young would have been consumed by the flames along with the aphids. The blackish-brown earwigs eat aphids too, but you won't find them for sale at the nursery or embroidered on clothing.

Nor will you find the black widow embellishing pockets and pocketbooks, though she is a beautiful spider, the glossy red and black of the ladybug in reverse. Supposedly black spiders bring bad luck and white spiders good, though when a small white spider ran across my hand on the porch yesterday, I did not feel kissed by fortune. The bright green and red stripes of the leafhopper or lovely blue eyes and wings of a bombardier beetle may charm us enough to forgive their six legs, but nothing entices us to exonerate eight. Consider the *Argiope aurantia*, one of our most colorful spiders, the big garden orb weaver children call the writing spider for the bold white zigzags of stabilimenta the nearly inconsequential male spins through the middle of her web; the sight of her handsome striped legs and bold black, gold, and white markings causes an arachnophobic shudder.

My son was twelve the summer I spent photographing the invertebrates in my garden, and when I projected my slides for him and his friends, my subjects, big as the horror film creepy-crawlies, filled the kids with glee. They cheered what they termed "raw, predatory evil" on the face of the green lynx spider and applauded the huge, notched black eyes of the wasp. Supposedly we fear insects not because our ancestors believed they caused plagues, but because they look like robots, because their exoskeletons make them resemble machines, and nearly all of our depictions of Martians resemble insects; they are so alien, so other. But when I made myself look through the lens at the faces of the creatures from my yard, they didn't appear machine-like at all. Instead they seemed oddly recognizable, in a strange way almost human in their solemn concentration on the task that is their lives. I've read that yellow jackets are so smart they habituate parking lots in the deep south, waiting for incoming cars because the bugs killed on those windshields and grills will be fresher. How smart, I wonder, is the spider?

Who knows? Not even a sharp micro lens could reveal all the secrets of my house and my yard. A miniscule leafhopper sings in my black-eyed susans, though I can't hear him, for the sound doesn't travel through the air, only through the leaves and stems from one leafhopper to another. While I sleep earwigs climb the woody stalks of my roses to eat the giant willow aphids; unseen by me the bat that lives in the box on the side of my garage glides after the tobacco fly flitting through the dark. The larvae of the leatherwings devour tiny grasshopper eggs inside the earth while wolf spiders dance in courtship and line their burrows. And hidden in the corners of my basement and garage the black widow crouches inside her web, combing her strong silk.

As a child I read mysteries because I believed I lived in a world without them. My suburban street seemed so ordinary, so predictable, so sanitized and stripped, I thought nothing lay hidden. Or perhaps that is what I was told. It was the 1950s; my parents and their neighbors, children of the Depression, were still celebrating the end of the world war. Civilization had been saved, good had triumphed over evil, which seemed also to mean that cleanliness had triumphed over filth. The world pictured in my mother's old photograph album, with its funny clothes and old-fashioned cars, was history. We were modern, living in the age of antibiotics and shampoo. And though the bright safety of our new order was boring, through it I learned to fear the dark shadows we'd escaped, everything I felt so securely protected from by time or space. Some claim the idea of the world before we were born evokes terror because it is so indifferent to our existence it is unaware of our absence. So is the natural world we inhabit indifferent to our desires, but I was young enough then to believe that all the creatures I feared bore me malice. And though it is surely not malice but that indifference we fear, even as adults the very words we use deny it. The spider carries venom; she is not indifferent, she is *venomous*.

What I discovered when I took a close look at the hidden world all around me is that each of its creatures is as serious about its life as I am about mine. We do not question that mammals have feelings. The giant ape was in love, so Hollywood tells us. We own dogs and cats and see for ourselves what makes them sad or happy. We witness their elation and on occasion their grief; they don't need words to express emotion. And yet we give them words. Every one of my dogs has had a voice, which was my voice, made cute, as I spoke for them. Once, after a student scoffed when my husband confided to a class that his dog had a voice, the other students admitted, one by one, that they too gave their dogs voices. To say that we anthropomorphize our pets and dehumanize our enemies is to state the obvious. Only the narrated life speaks to us.

Does an ant feel joy at the sight of a bread crumb; can a spider mourn? These are the questions Jeffrey Moussaieff Masson and Susan McCathy ask in *When Elephants Weep*, their anecdotal argument for the emotional lives of animals: does a spider love its babies? There are female spiders who sacrifice their lives for their young, breaking down their own organs to nourish their eggs. A wolf spider who loses her egg sac will pick up and carry an empty snail shell, a bit of fluff, or even a rabbit dropping, as if to hold onto what it once promised. Instinct or love? I can't say. I don't speak for the spider, though surely outside of the articulated world of our human concerns the distinction makes no difference at all.

MORNING LIGHT

———

I.

IT BEGINS IN DARKNESS. Before dawn, before the laughing gulls wake, before the Governor Edward Hyde, which departs the island for Swan Quarter at 6:30 every morning, sends a smudge of smoke skyward and sounds its deep horn. While the hull of the moon is still caught in a black sky freighted with stars. At the ocean, breakers will be spilling their thunderous white spume, but here at the harbor the water is glass, a bottomless sheen the color of jet. Already there is a faint bluing at the horizon across the harbor; the sky's black ink is dissolving into indigo, its brilliant plot of stars disappearing. The light is as swift as a swallow. You cannot go to it; you must wait for it to come to you.

Always I am up early here. For years I have crept through a dark cottage and across the screened porch with my camera and tripod to wait on a deck built high above a shelf of shallow water across from the Coast Guard station just inside the harbor. Nearly always it is May, and though the summer season is another one, two, or three weeks away, vacationers have begun to crowd the village. By noon the road from the ferry dock to the foot of the harbor will clog with bicyclists and pedestrians strolling from motel to museum to the Slushy Stand and shops, the Pelican and Jolly Roger, but at this hour I am the only visitor awake. Hidden inside the sleeve of night, I might be a spy. All photographers are spies.

Across the harbor, below the widening scrim of blue, a band the color of brick spreads along the rim of the land and low cluster of buildings. The water stirs with the faint sound of a motor as a crab boat putters toward the Sound; the darkness has thinned just enough for me to make out the crossbars in the stern and the crabber standing at the throttle in his yellow rain bibs. When he reaches the channel at the mouth of the harbor, the engine roars to life and the boat spurts past the rocks into the great basin of water that lies between here and the mainland twenty-three miles away. At the fishing shack next door, once Sam Jones' dock house, another motor begins its low rumble. Just as the skiff pulls away, a dog leaps from the dock into the bow, startling a great egret feeding in the shallows. The bird emits an irritated croak and takes flight with the sound of an umbrella opening. O'cockers, these commercial fishermen are called, hoi-toiders for a brogue that dates back to Elizabethan England, practitioners of a way of life that is rapidly being supplanted by sportfishing and eco-tours, just as their red and white wooden skiffs have been replaced by fiberglass in the last decade.

Along the edge of the harbor, called Silver Lake, though to the O'cockers it is neither the harbor nor Silver Lake but the

Creek, a scattering of motels occupies the space where seine nets once hung to dry. The new nets, nylon and polypropylene, are left heaped in the boats or near the docks with their pocked floats of orange and yellow closed-cell foam. The fisherman gliding toward the channel, retriever posed like a figurehead at the prow, will use an electric reel to troll the Atlantic for Spanish mackerel. When he passes on his way back into the harbor, he will call up to me, then reach into the bottom of his boat and fling me a fish, the Spanish long and graceful, glinting white and yellow as it swims through the clean morning air. I will fillet it and put it in the refrigerator for dinner while the sun is still kissing the screens at the windows of the bedrooms where my husband and son lie sleeping.

The sunrise is beside the point. Once, at the Grand Canyon, I rose more than an hour before dawn to station myself at Mather Point, wedging my tripod into a crevice between a boulder and the guardrail while it was still so dark that I could not tell the sky from the abyss, shooting four, five, or six rolls of film as the sky woke from periwinkle to magenta, then fire and gold, and the canyon emerged from night's black cave into tiers of jagged purple shadow. Just as the sun was about to lift above the rim, a vanload of tourists swarmed the overlook. Within seconds the sun cleared the canyon wall, pouring a sheet of glaring white light over the point and washing the color from the rock. The visitors clapped, and with a few snaps of their pocket cameras they were gone, morning cousins of the snowbirds who pack Mallory Square on Key West to cheer the sun into the sea every evening. I crossed the empty ledge and aimed my camera westward while honey-colored tentacles of light pulled stripes and pockets of the cracked-open land from its plum-colored vault. Candy light, the great landscape photographer Carr Clifton calls it.

Here on Ocracoke the rising sun sends a shaft of orange across the water, silhouetting two fishermen in a net boat.

Some mornings I trap its fire behind a low cloud of lavender just as it traces the puffing at the upper edge with flame, gilding the harbor and streaking the sky. Others the sky is plumed with clouds that ignite along the bottom. Sometimes there is only cirrus filmy as peach and mauve chiffon, but if the day is cloudless by the time the sun climbs above the wall of live oak and cedar beside the Anchorage Inn it will have paled to a yellow-white flare that trails sunspots across my lens and bleaches out the sky. Once the sun has risen, the place to be is on the other side of the harbor, Around Creek, where the tender morning light laps against the sailboats at anchor, warming their white hulls, the painted white bricks of the lighthouse, and the gables of the Barksdale house, rising from its wreath of peppervine behind a row of private docks whose weathered gray wood the early sun tints hazel. To the northwest the Coast Guard Station glistens behind the Community Store dock, where masts as tall as tapers dip a wobble of lines into a shining pastel sea. Stand in the same place at noon, beneath the tyrannical light of midday, and the scene turns hard and flat, not worth the price of a single roll of film, though that is the way most visitors will view it.

And I am grateful to them, for always I am alone with the morning on this island, here at the harbor, in the salt meadow and marshes off South Point Road, wading into the warm shallows at Teach's Hole, where a rookery in the hammock sends a stream of white ibises across a china blue sky, or at the North End, where the gulls flutter and cry behind the Chicamacomico making its way across the inlet to Hatteras, on the ridge of the dune where the light ripens in the sea oats and turns the sand a pale pink, or at the ragged line where the surf breaks on the beach as the sun pulls itself up from the ocean, a ball of fire ninety-three million miles and so many light years away it is impossible to comprehend how old this new light really is.

The calculations make my head spin. Even the reference librarian gets it wrong. By his math, on the day this light set out from the sun the earth was still in the Ice Age. Woolly mammoths and saber-toothed tigers roamed North America, where man had just arrived, trudging across the Bering Land Bridge from Asia. New England and the upper Midwest lay frozen beneath a glacier, and the Outer Banks, this narrow ribbon of sand off the coast of North Carolina, were still mainland, a ridge upon a vast coastal plain more than twenty miles from the sea. And by the time I find out that he is wrong, his miscalculations have become my facts. I want to believe that it has taken this light thirty thousand years to reach me, to imagine how it traveled all those millennia without pause, for as it spins it is the earth that creates its own darkness. The only difference between the soft light of morning and the steely light of noon is the angle of vision.

It is less difficult to comprehend the age of the land, for it is there beneath my feet even when I cannot see it, its own proof that it has not sprung from nothing but endured. The earth has weight and surface; I can take a piece of it in my hand or fill a vial with this sand and carry it back across the Sound inside my pocket. But though I walk upon the land, what I see is landscape, which is not the land itself but the interaction of land and light, and what I photograph is not the weight and surface of the earth but the light that it reflects. When I try to take that light in hand, it slips between my fingers; if I put it in my pocket, darkness closes in. To make a photograph is always an attempt to hold that which cannot be held, to keep that which cannot be kept, to preserve, to save, to make permanent the passing of a moment. It's the hedging of a bet against memory's faulty circuits. Each year I return to this island because I have found something here I did not know I'd lost and do not wish to lose again. I photograph its landscape

because to do so is a ritual in paying attention. Like the
sunrise, the pictures are beside the point, not because I have
already made so many, drawer after file drawer of transparen-
cies in archival sheets, portfolios of prints, albums full of snapshots, but because the island has etched itself into my memory,
not in the power of recall but as a presence that lives inside my
body. It is printed on the lining of my eyelids and collected on
my skin; my nostrils hold its salt, my tongue its windy damp-
ness; the willets nesting in the marsh call inside my ear. I carry
its landscape with me even when I am not there.

2.

I CAME TO OCRACOKE for the first time in the summer of
1972. My first husband and I had set up camp for the month
on Hatteras Island, at Rodanthe, which was then just a fishing pier, restaurant, mom and pop motel, and the brand new
cinder block showers of the KOA—hard to imagine now
that Rodanthe looks like a theme park and Route 12 like the
commercial strip leading into any mid-sized city. Hatteras then
was much like Ocracoke now, for outside the village the entire
island of Ocracoke is protected by the National Park Service.
From the Hatteras ferry at the North End to the ferry dock
in the village, its thirteen miles of Route 12 travel a topog-
raphy so unencroached that in the mornings one can often
spot a pair of oystercatchers strutting along the saddle of the
dunes. More than once I have stopped my car in the middle
of the highway, turning off the ignition to steady a long lens
on a beanbag laid across the window. Sand dribbles across the
pavement, and the only hint of human habitation is the hum
of the electric lines that run along the highway. One drought-
stricken year they sparked a wildfire in the marsh; as my
ferry approached I watched a small plane sucking water from
Pamlico Sound. When I went up in a plane myself the next

day, the big blackened patches were raw sores, though a year later they had healed as the land renewed itself. The first time I crossed the seven tidal creeks, their names a poem I know by heart—Island, Shad Hole, Old Hammock, Molasses, Quokes Point, Parkers, Try Yard—the highway was little more than ten years old, the first stretch of pavement in the village barely over twenty. I still have a few faded slides of the beach and Silver Lake before the water tower and new motels gave it a skyline, but no memory of my impression. The following summer, when we returned, we passed from ferry to ferry, traveling from Hatteras to Cedar Island without stopping, driving the scenic route from Richmond, Virginia to South Carolina's Grand Strand and Charleston.

I did not return again until the spring of 1990, when a group of my students rented a cottage for the weekend and we held our last workshop at the beach. That fall I came back with my husband and son to visit friends in the small cottage at Windmill Point that I would return to for many years. Its appeal is location, not comfort. During World War II it was a barracks at the naval station that operated on the other side of the harbor; the big wraparound screened porch and deck were added when it was moved to Down Point for a fishing shack. Inside it has a shipshape look, with ceilings of knotty pine and two bedrooms barely large enough for a pair of twin beds each. The owner has framed the window at the end of the small living-dining room with shelves that hold a set of glass dishes and the same collection of tattered paperbacks and faded jigsaw puzzles that can be found in every cottage on the island. There are two rickety wooden folding chairs that can be pulled up to an equally rickety gateleg table, a bench with three thin foam cushions, and an armchair with a broken spring. All four mattresses are furrowed; one of the bedframes lists above an impaired leg. The first time my husband and I made breakfast

we fouled the rooms with an unspeakable stench and found
a melted rubber Batman on the bottom of the toaster oven.
Occasionally the tides deposit a bloated, reeking fish beneath
the house; at night, big black palmetto bugs crawl up through
the pipes and huddle near the drains. But we sleep to the
sound of Silver Lake lapping against the pilings underneath us
and wake to the cry of gulls and a salty breeze wafting through
the open windows. When I come back from the beach each
morning, I wash the sand from my hair in a wooden shower
stall at the end of the deck, where I can watch the harbor
traffic as barn swallows dip and turn around me, flashing their
golden bellies. It's heaven.

I resumed photography about the same time that I returned
to Ocracoke, having given it up shortly after the time I first
visited nearly twenty years before. I had begun making photographs when I was a junior in college, the same year I signed
up for a class in writing fiction, though I would not have
known that photography was a class one could take had not
one of my suitemates taken it the year before. I didn't even
own a camera, but I bought an inexpensive twin-lens reflex
and prowled the streets. Like many young photographers, I
was smitten with Diane Arbus, whose exposé of the grotesque
inside the ordinary life of the middle class is irresistible to
a jaundiced teenaged eye. For a time I dated a grad student
who shot landscapes, but as a subject the land did not engage
me then. Although I admired Ansel Adams, the Midwestern
landscape around me lacked the drama of Yosemite or a
moonrise over Hernandez. I was a city kid. The rolling hills
of Indiana's limestone country were pretty enough, but pretty
was not what I wanted. In my attempt to emulate the seeming
matter-of-factness of Arbus's voyeurism (which was of course
anything but matter-of-fact) and reductive focus of her vision,
I looked for the debased, diseased, and deformed. Like most

novices, I thought photographs were all about their subjects. It did not occur to me, nor did anyone tell me, that photography is about light. It is about light in the same way literature is about language. Though I made a few good pictures, enough to exhibit and win an occasional award, I knew scarcely more about what I was doing when I stopped than when I started.

I quit because I was poor. At the time I was printing color, then more expensive than black and white. I had run out of paper and gone to the store for a new box, but when I saw the price, in one of those flashes of self-knowledge that occasionally overtake the young, I understood that almost none of the photographs I had made was worth the paper it was printed on. There was nothing technically wrong with them—I was a good printer, and I had mastered the chromogenic print's painstaking formula of addition and subtraction—but I didn't know why I was using color any more than I had known why I used black and white. It was simply the next level in the classes I had taken. My images were routine. Anyone could have made them; there was nothing compelling in my vision. I wasn't an artist—I couldn't draw, I couldn't paint, I had no visual training. Nor could I pretend to be practicing a trade. I not only wasn't making money with my camera, I wasn't even trying. I was writing fiction, which seemed a more affordable art. Typing paper was cheap. It didn't matter if *The New Yorker* and *Esquire* didn't want my stories; it didn't cost me much to write them. I put my camera away and enrolled in a graduate writing program. But I had no idea on the day that I left the big communal darkroom at VCU in Richmond, a room whose murky shadows and amber glow were as familiar to me as my kitchen, that more than twenty years would elapse before I entered another.

By the time I picked up my camera again, I was middle-aged and comfortably middle class. I had published my fiction after all and established myself as a teacher of writing. So it would seem purely a coincidence of economics that Ocracoke should lie at either end of that long hiatus. And yet I had come to the Outer Banks in 1972 with the intention to take pictures, for a friend of a friend had an advertising agency that had done some work for the National Park Service, and I set off with a vague assurance that if I got any good pictures of birds, the Park Service might want them, though the longest lens I owned had a focal length of 105 millimeters and no birds seemed inclined to come within its range. That was the last summer I attempted to make photographs, for I felt as if I'd failed an assignment. A decade later, when my son was born, I bought a point-and-shoot. Only when I went back to Ocracoke with my workshop in the spring of 1990 did I take my old Nikon out of the closet, perhaps because I'd just finished a novel about a photographer and writing it had made me nostalgic for the smell of the darkroom and the way the photographer stalks the world. One of my students also brought her camera. She was not a photographer by training, but her pictures proved so much more carefully composed than mine I was ashamed. It didn't matter that my training had been more in name than fact—for in the 1960s the prevailing pedagogy in art was "go and do," and the only actual words of instruction I remember are "The darkroom's across the hall." That September, when I went back to Ocracoke with my husband and son I had even more reason to want to please myself, for in the summer of 1990 my second novel, ten years in the writing, had been rejected by my publisher. When our hostess bragged about the secondhand teleconverter she'd picked up for ten dollars, doubling the length of her 100-millimeter lens and allowing her to shoot birds, it seemed a small price to pay for a little artistic redemption. It turned out that the camera store didn't have a used teleconverter to fit, but for a hundred dollars the dealer sold me a used 400-millimeter lens. That winter, in the Everglades on our way to visit my husband's brother, I focused on a white ibis just as a drop of silver water fell from the red, decurved bill into a still pool in Taylor Slough and was hooked.

3.

TO MAKE A PHOTOGRAPH you must learn how to read light. You must develop a feel for its chemistry, its texture and color; its purity must become palpable to you. But to read light is to experience ephemerality, to know your own mortality, the fleeting nature of all things. One winter dusk during the many years we spent Christmas in Florida, as I strolled with my husband along Deerfield Beach, a banner of light the color of burnt sugar lay unfurled along the horizon, separating the deep teal of the sky from the verdigris of the ocean, a palette at once so subtle and intense I longed to bolt back to our room to fetch my camera, though I spoil so many walks that way I promised myself that I would wait and capture it the next evening. But of course the light is never the same, and in the morning when I read the paper, I discovered that burnt sugar was exactly what that smoky sienna band along the horizon had been. A swath of wildfires had consumed the sugar cane fields in the islands to the south. And though a scorched smell still lingered in the air, the fires were out. You cannot make today's photograph tomorrow, just as tomorrow you will no longer be what you were today.

My husband does not read light. To him one dusk is as exquisite as the next; he sees no difference whether I reach my subject in the buttery light of an early summer evening or the impossible glare of noon. To walk the cliffs above the Pacific on a late summer afternoon when the light saps the landscape of its color and blinds my lens seems no less desirable to him than to linger while the rocky seaside warms and the dying sun stains the ocean. My disappointments puzzle. My pokiness annoys. "You've got enough pictures, let's go," he says invariably just as the light sweetens. I can't blame him. It's no fun to travel with an addict. Like all addictions, photography is a solitary sport.

And so, while he sleeps, I slip from our bed into the maw of night to wait the morning. I trap rabbits in my headlights, raccoons, opossums, now and then a fox; deer spring across the road before me. Once at Merritt Island National Wildlife Refuge, positioning myself for a sunshot mist rising off the marsh, I waded into the reeds beside the road at 5 a.m. and heard the warning stomp and hiss of an alligator in the ditch At the Lower Suwannee Refuge an alligator charges my four-wheel-drive, tail lashing so furiously as he runs I think he is a dervish; it's no exaggeration that they gallop. I've watched one eat a coot, seen a crocodile devour a jacana. In Costa Rica a bull with horns like scythes emerges from the morning fog with the suddenness of a drunk driver, and as I back away he raises his head into a startled stare.

In the Rocky Mountains I maneuver a rental car up dirt-road switchbacks at the edge of a cliff in the dark; in the Smokies I slip on wet rocks beside a raging river. At the Santee Wildlife Refuge the dark swamp chirrs with hidden menace while branches snare my clothing and webs trawl at my face and I swear no sunset picture is worth this prickling terror, though the next night I am back. As dusk settles on Virginia's Back Bay a snipe's wing brushes through my hair; at Cumberland Falls it's bats. More than once I have accidentally locked myself into the wilderness of a wildlife refuge overnight. And one breathtaking morning in Mason County, Michigan, I follow a winding path up through a woods so wet and green and diaphanous with mist that I forget I am a sitting duck, a woman alone who has left her car at a deserted rest stop.

The photographs are stunning. It doesn't matter that they will be hidden away in drawers. It is the act of making them, the act of writing, that matters—the act of living, I remind myself, and not the life.

4.

I LEARNED TO READ LIGHT because there was a time when I needed to be without language, when I needed to travel back to that place where nothing is named and we dream in pure light and color. When I failed to publish my second novel, I believed that words had failed me, and I didn't want to write another just because I was expected to. If I was to write again, it would be because I needed words, not because I was a writer.

I did not write for two years. Then I wrote another novel, and when it was done I failed to publish that one too.

How, without whining, is one to describe the way her world dims? It's as if she's been a member of a club; then one day she tries the clubhouse door to find the lock has been changed. "You write well, but you won't sell," editors and agents tell her. "Today's reader wants a high concept plot and an upbeat message. Your work is literary. It's dark, but not Oprah dark. There's no market." But when she repeats the things they say, the words sound false. After all, some literary fiction still gets published. There's no lack of grim novels on the bookstore shelves. So everyone knows—her colleagues, her department head, her dean, her students, or maybe it's herself who knows—that she must deserve her luck; her work must be no good. She doesn't get raises; invitations to read stop coming in; she has to fight for a promotion that comes years too late. Because she needs the money, she teaches summer school instead of writing. When her students and colleagues win grants and awards, she offers congratulations; when they complain about sub rights, pub dates, sales, reviews, or page design, she commiserates; but her heart is black.

Think of war, she tells herself sternly, think of natural disasters, others endure so much worse, think of famine, think of murder or the random cruelty of disease, do not wallow. But the language of luck has no power of persuasion. Good or bad, it's all clichés.

And so I taught myself to speak another tongue. For a decade marked by the faltering of my career, my father's suicide, my son's troubled adolescence, the decline of our remaining parents, friendships lost to midlife crises, others lost to death, and the sudden irreversibility of aging, I made photographs.

Some were published, some were purchased, many hung in shows. For six months a series made on Ocracoke lined the hallways of the David Williams House, the Ocracoke Preservation Society Museum. When it was time to take the exhibit down, I traveled to the island to attend the village Christmas party. The village was quiet; most of the restaurants and motels had closed for the season. At the Island Ragpicker I bought my Christmas presents half price. A cold front was moving in, and at the end of the docks gulls puffed and huddled. Near the tall fishing shack a great blue heron fed in the shallows—one rarely sees a great blue on Ocracoke in May, for they leave the island to breed. The constellations in the dome of the sky had shifted; the sun set not behind the Coast Guard Station, where I expected it, but near the lighthouse, streaking the heavens with ridges of violet and gold, as if the clarity of the winter light allowed me to see all the way to the mountains. When it was dark, I walked along the village lanes looking at the Christmas lights that seemed to be strung into the sky, where they mingled with stars such as I never see at

home, though by morning rain had come, and the world had
been swallowed by heavy gray clouds. Angry waves crested
and spilled in the harbor, the boats heaved on their anchors,
and the wind drove so sharp and wet I could not walk along
the beach. There was nothing to do but read inside my small
and spartan room. Still, I was glad to be there, because that is
where I learned to look at darkness and see light.

5.

IT HAS BEEN YEARS now since I have stayed at Windmill
Point. For a decade my husband and son no longer came
to Ocracoke. My son has grown and gone, and though my
husband enjoyed watching the black skimmers on the tidal
flat and redwing blackbirds in the marsh, he never loved the
island as I do; for him it was a place of day-old ball scores and
bad weather. The last year I stayed there I stayed alone, and
then because there was no phone and it seemed unnecessary
to rent an entire cottage for one person, because I grew too
busy to plan far enough ahead and instead just stole away, I
moved from Around Creek to the Silver Lake Motel, where
I watched the harbor every morning and evening from an
observation deck up a steep circular staircase from a second
floor porch that offered a roof when there was rain. Year after
year Ed Wrobleski, the burly proprietor, who sat on the porch
at the top of the steps just outside the office door, greeted me
with the words, "There's a breeze," as he tipped his face back
to savor the salt air. Then one winter his wife died; when I
came back the next spring he was gone too, and when his heirs
doubled the rates and turned my porch into a bar, I moved
to the Island Inn. Until the harbor was dredged for the naval
base in the decade before World War II, the land in front of
the Island Inn was marsh, but now the view of the Creek is
eclipsed by the new two-story Ride the Wind. Even the open

strip of sand at the foot of Silver Lake, where I often set up my tripod in the evenings, is closed off. A new marina is in place, and the network of docks is fenced off with no-trespassing signs. From the ferry, far out in Pamlico Sound, when the first shimmer of land appears, a thin, dark thread at the horizon, a shadow upon the sea so faint it might be an apparition, it is no longer the lighthouse that confirms the sighting but the water and cell phone towers.

Perhaps because change came so slowly in the past, I failed to foresee just what kind of record I would make when I began to photograph the island. It was 1938 before electricity arrived; until 1956, the only phone was at the Coast Guard station. At the beginning of the '80s islanders still collected rainwater in cisterns for drinking. Still, I might have guessed. Even in 1990, the village I'd first seen in 1972 was barely recognizable, for once the water tower was built, development exploded. Already the incongruous brick Anchorage Inn had heaved up its four stories on the bank of the harbor, and the village had grown suburbs, great cottages that sleep twelve and more crowding up against the marshes. By 1991 Papa Howard's, the big old island house with a crooked chimney that my students and I rented for pennies in 1990, was a chic shop full of windchimes and handmade tscotchkes. A few years later as the Cedar Island ferry chugged into Silver Lake I spotted new green shingles and freshly painted trim on the dormers of Sam Jones' Castle, the derelict cedar-shake mansion that had presided over the bottom of the harbor vacant, leaking, and for sale ever since Sam Jones was buried with his horse in the woods near Springer's Point. Where gaillardia and pennywort used to push up through the sandy cracks of his cement parking pad there was a lawn so green it looked radioactive. Next door the old fisherman's motel had been torn down, in its place a brand new inn with private balconies, aqua vinyl siding, and a fancy wedding tent out front. O'Neal's Dockside, where my son used to buy bait, is no longer dockside but relocated to the highway, and the wooden archway on the dock that advertised blood-worms and fresh mullet has lost a leg and faded. The harbor and the creeks are jammed with neon-colored kayaks, and the beaches where I used to walk for hours without encountering another person are crisscrossed with the tracks of four-wheel drives. The Coast Guard station is empty, its crew sent to Hatteras; from the lookout tower, once as trim and white as a sail, aluminum siding in pied shades of gray and dirty white flaps loose. The cedar shakes of the fishing shack at Windmill Point have been re-faced with planks the raw red color of the clay soil back in the Piedmont, and between it and my beloved cottage, where a pastel wooden skiff used to lie rotting in the sand beside a pile of crab traps, there is a brand new dock with a fancy screened gazebo.

An island is not meant for progress. To watch an island be developed is to know your own diminishment, to mark the years off your life like days on a calendar, to count not what has been added but what has been lost.

And yet in the mornings, when I watch the fishing skiffs glide toward the Ditch at the mouth of Silver Lake, when I ride my bike through the clear and sparkling air around the curve of marsh past Back Road to Up Trent and see the fiddler crabs scatter as I cross the little creek, when I pedal Down Point and coast past the ibises bobbing in the boggy light-house yard, past Styron's Store, and around the loop where the chickens behind a little white house with a porch swing set up a squawk from their pen next to the family graveyard, when I follow an overgrown path through the woods among the graves that are tucked everywhere in the village, for Ocracoke is a place where death is just another part of life and the dead are not banished to their own city, when I walk the grassy lane at the end of the fork off South Point Road through the marsh into the Sound and the terns wheel and cry overhead, or when I come up over the dune and the untamed beach spreads before me, a blue ocean churning at my feet, I feel such happiness, such joy in the body of the earth, I listen close and feel its spangled heart beat.

THE WEDDING PAGES

———

My son and a friend from high school days are on the deck drinking a beer to fortify themselves for a wedding. The friend's suit is draped over a living room chair—they have yet to dress, though it's 1:45 and the wedding is at 2. The suit needs cleaning, he observes as they come inside; it's been to three weddings in the past three weeks. Upstairs my son's comes out of the dry cleaner's plastic. Later he will hang it up. Such tidiness is not like him, but it has to travel to another wedding this month. He's lost weight in the near decade since high school, when we bought the suit for his prom, to which he took this friend's brother's girlfriend, also a friend, because—well, it's complicated, but isn't everything? Since then he's had the suit tailored for another wedding, and the fit isn't bad, though he's sloshing around in the size 16 quadruple-E dress shoes we bought to go with it. (Down from the size eighteen chucks he wore for everyday, thanks to proper fitting. He's a big boy, six feet eight to be exact.) The shoes had to be ordered, of course. He didn't want them, but he could hardly wear the expensive suit with his crusty high-tops, and, as I pointed out, he would need them later, when he graduated, when he got married, when he interviewed for a job. Not to worry, he assured me, he had no plans to do any of those things. And when I laugh about that now—he's graduated twice, I remind him, from high school *and* from college and worn the shoes to both events—he reminds me that none of the weddings he has worn them to were his, and he has yet to attend a job interview in a suit. True. He writes for and edits a fishing tabloid that comes out of Wilmington, North Carolina, a job he loves, even if the summer season is too busy, and for the interview a pair of waders and bait-stained T-shirt probably would have done just fine. All the same, he goes to a lot weddings, he wears the shoes, those investments in the future, though apparently his feet have shrunk; he's now a fifteen double-E, which certainly makes life easier, at least when it comes to shopping.

Summer season he works long hours seven days a week, and so this Labor Day weekend the bride and groom have chosen is the first time I've seen my son in months. Last January a car hit him while he was riding his bicycle and shattered his right leg below the knee, this just after he shed the boot and crutches he'd been using since he broke his ankle in November. All winter I was back and forth with food, but the leg has healed, though it still swells from knee to toes, and by the time the reception is over the oversized right dress shoe should fit just fine.

When he was a baby I used to hold that same foot in the palm of my hand, marveling at how small it was, how pink and perfect. That was when the whole of him fit the length of arm between my wrist and elbow. "Look at his little feet," I would crow. "They'll never be this clean again." These days his uncle, also a fisherman—that is, a man accustomed by trade to gore— says he can't bear to look. The scars where the pins were put into Max's ankle run up and down each side like little laces. There are circles that look like cigarette burns where a metal fixator was screwed to his leg until the tibia could be stabilized within by a titanium rod. Road burns and lacerations. My son loves his bicycles nearly as much as he loves his boat. He has a lot of scars.

"Where's Dad?" he says now. There is an unfamiliar urgency in his voice, unfamiliar because my son is not a worrier, worries about so little in fact that he once asked if I thought he ought to worry about that. His friends worry all the time, he said. As for Dad, not here, gone for a run or something, I don't know.

"Oh," Max says. "I was hoping he could help me with my tie." The irony that my son has mastered more complicated fishing knots than most fishermen he knows but cannot tie a tie is not lost on him, though the notion that perhaps he should have asked Dad to stick around is. The Catholic church where the wedding will be held is just around the corner, but it's ten til, and suddenly I, who thought I knew all I need to know about ties—I know silks, I know design, I chose every single one of the extensive collection of gorgeous ties in my husband's closet, one of which is dangling uselessly from my son's hand—am on the internet, googling how to tie a tie.

"I must have skipped that class in mom school," I joke over my shoulder, but whoa—that was not one class, I must have slept through a whole semester. There are four-in-hands, Grantchesters, Plattsburghs, Pratts, Hanovers, Victorias,

Kelvins, Orientals. The Cavendish knot, I learn, was named for two Cambridge University physicists who worked in the Cavendish labs and developed more than eighty different ways to tie a tie—this is what they do in physics lab? There are only thirteen ways to count a blackbird and fifty ways to leave your lover, but more than eighty ways to tie a tie and ten minutes til the wedding. I click on the four-in-hand—it's the easiest, the website promises, the bird in hand worth two in the bush, but it looks *terrible* in the picture. Windsor sounds familiar, half Windsor even better since it must be only half as hard, right? oh but no, the Windsor and half Windsor each have thirteen steps, *thirteen steps to tie a tie,* and I can't even loop my strap in yoga class, but wait, here comes Dad, home just in time, back from walking the dogs, our hero of the paisleys, regimentals, pin dots and repps, foulards and jacquards, the Jerry Garcias, Liberty of Londons, Lily Dachés, and Chevaliers, and off they go, the two young men once boys, all tied up, to watch their friend get married.

The groom, let's call him Don since he deserves to have his privacy protected, is marrying the first girl my son ever kissed. This Max has confided in a moment of uncustomary candor— we didn't know he'd ever had a date until one New Year's Day, when a girl came strolling out of his room to brush her teeth at noon. (He's not a thing like his older brother, my stepson, who both worries and confides.) But my son and his friend are not here for the bride, they've come to support the groom, who once shared a house with Max while Max was still in college.

I, of course, am not invited. But as I've said, the big Gothic church where the wedding will take place is just around the corner, and in the course of a Saturday's errands I've happened upon many a bridal party making its grand entrance or adjourning. I could take a walk, but that's a little obvious, and anyway I can't walk. I'm the one with a bum leg now. My

left knee is sprained—hit by a dog the week before—actually
it's broken, but I don't know that yet, and so I'm still in the
"immobilizer," the soft cast with splints that runs from crotch
to ankle; I can drive, the orthopedist tells me, as long as I don't
have a clutch and can get into my car. It's an acrobatic feat, but
I've done it, and so at 2 p.m. I grab my keys and head to the
Bestway for a baguette because we really do need the bread
for dinner and the route takes me past the church, where sure
enough the pretty, dark-haired bride is tripping up the walk
with her army of attendants, all in red satin tea-length dresses
with red stiletto heels.

Wow, I think, they're still doing that, those satin dyed-to-
match shoes. I remember them from my high school prom and
my first wedding. They used to be a spring and summer staple
in the windows of the shoe stores, a single white satin heel on
a white cardboard riser, flanked by a rainbow of dyed pumps
and a promise that the shop could match any color. Pink, lilac,
lemon, aqua, baby blue, mint green. In those days no designer
would have offered bridesmaids' dresses in red—red was the
color of bordellos—and not even guests would have shown up
at a wedding wearing black—they might as well have come
bearing funeral wreaths and sympathy cards. But now red and
black both are popular choices for bridesmaids. Dark red, deep
red, sangria, apple, ruby, crimson, carnelian, lipstick, fire engine,
coral. At my first wedding, which was in the fall, my attendants
wore gold chiffon, "harvest gold," the yellowed clipping pasted
into my photo album says. Like refrigerators, like stoves. It was
that era.

It's a girl thing, I guess, this desire to see the bride in her
gown and her choice of bridesmaids' dresses, held over from
those days of green and gold appliances and pastel satin shoes,
since I am hardly a girl anymore. ("Imagine!" my mother says,
"my kids are senior citizens.") I won't talk to my son again until

tomorrow, and if I asked what style of dress the bride selected, if she had a veil, or what shade the bridesmaids' raiments were, he would look at me as if I were insane and say, "I don't know," which is to say he will not notice. In short, if I want to know, this little act of espionage is essential. Newspapers left off the elaborate descriptions of the gown and flowers years ago, not to mention that many brides forego the newspaper announcement altogether; these days the pictures are more likely to turn up online. Still I check out Sunday's paper.

At the breakfast table (breakfast for my son, a late lunch for me) I mention that there wasn't an announcement on the wedding page, and he looks at me as if I am insane. "I didn't even know the paper had a wedding page," he says. So I pass it over. It isn't what it was back in the reign of the Society Editor of course, back in the days when a society column observed the comings and goings of the local elite and the weddings ran for pages; it's called "Celebrations" now, and this Sunday's page features more anniversary couples than brides, including a couple who are celebrating their seventieth.

"Hmm," he says as he skims it. "It's like the obituary page."

"Well, not exactly," I protest with a laugh, but he's serious. The pictures on the wedding page may be bigger, they may be more attractive, but the pages perform exactly the same function: they notify readers of important passages in people's lives that would not otherwise be news. And I have to admit he's got a point. All practicality, my son is not much for the niceties we tend to hide behind, those doilies used to disguise the nicks and stains that make up much of life. Maybe it's a guy thing, but he looks at the wood and ignores the tatting.

I would like to think that I do too, but already I'm distracted, intrigued by the seventieth anniversary couple, who may be a whole lot closer in years to the obit page than the weddings, but by God they're both here, they're still celebrating. Which is the seventieth in the scheme of things, I wonder. For our twenty-fifth, a few years ago, I gave my husband a new wallet with a silver dollar tucked inside.

He liked the wallet, but when he saw the dollar, which cost considerably more than a dollar of course, he said, "What's this?"

"It's a silver dollar," I said. He looked blank.

"*It's our silver anniversary,*" I said.

"Oh," he said. We'll both be elderly if we make it to our fiftieth, the golden, much too old for the big elaborate bash one's kids are supposed to host. My parents were divorced, and my husband's mother died before that burden fell to us. Parents of sons, no daughters, we've dodged the obligation to throw a big, expensive party.

Still, I'm curious: where do you go after gold?

Marriage.about.com actually lists the hundredth—it's the 10K diamond, by the way, just in case yours is coming up—but after the twentieth they start skipping, and the seventieth doesn't make the cut. The first is paper. I know because the wife of one of my husband's former students was so proud of the Cubs tickets she bought to commemorate their initial year together. I have no recollection of what I gave my first husband for our first anniversary. Happyanniversary.com suggests a love letter or a poem on pretty scented paper, or if you prefer the modern alternative, clocks. As in the clock is ticking? For the first year after I married my first husband, I climbed the stairs to bed every night with an acute awareness that my life had just grown one day shorter, with a gnawing sense that I was one day closer to my death. Something about getting married had made me feel the clock was running out.

We did not make it to our eleventh, the steel, though happyanniversary.com's recommendation for that is one of my favorites: "If your husband is a Pittsburgh Steelers fan, shopping should be a no-brainer." As for the husband hoping to find just the right piece of steel jewelry, "trust us, your wife will be just as happy with silver or gold." Who looks this stuff up? Except me, but I'm a writer, and so year by year I check my bygone anniversaries out. The thirteenth—you'd think it would be horseshoes or rabbits' feet, four-leaf clovers and lucky stars—is lace, as in lingerie.

"Many women love it," they report. "Some are ambivalent. Some really hate it. It would be impossible for us to tell you what category your wife fits into."

What I love about the site is its pitch of practicality *and* romance, which couples the suggestion of a woven willow basket and a picnic in the woods to mark the ninth (pottery) with a reminder not to forget the bug spray. It's the girl and guy thing together, which is what marriage is supposed to be all about, right, once you're past the girl thing of the wedding?

Or was, back in the days of the society editor, who had gone the way of the carriage return by the time *The New York Times* began covering commitment ceremonies and same-sex parties about love.

I've saved the descriptions of my first wedding. Announcements then were free; the society editor decided whose picture went top and center, who got the headline and who the footnote, that postage-stamp slot at the bottom of the page. In most newspapers these days the amount of ink you get for weddings and obituaries alike is the amount of money you decide to spend. But there I am top and center in both *The Youngstown Vindicator* and *The Hammond Times*, a position that had nothing to do with my pedigree and everything with the groom's. According to the *Times* I wore a floor-length gown of silk organza over taffeta trimmed with re-embroidered Alençon lace, whatever that is. The dress gets a whole paragraph and my "Edwardian bouquet," which I recall as a stumpy little lollipop tied up with a bow, along with my "forward headpiece of lace" and "silk illusion veil," another. Neither paper mentions the hundreds of tiny silk-covered buttons up the back, only the cathedral train that hid all the ones I left unbuttoned because I was running late. Those buttons are the only memory I have of the wedding, though everything went smoothly, the *Vindicator's* society columnist assures me, even if my ex-father-in-law wanted to shower us with Rice Krispies because he thought rice would be too harsh. This was apparently before birdseed became a popular alternative and long before the live butterfly release upped the ante. I don't know if Don and his bride had butterflies; my first husband and I were pelted with rice. In the little white wedding album that survived the marriage there is a picture in which we look like figures in a snow globe, though when I went looking for my wedding portrait, I found its folder stuffed with pages cut from an old album that belonged to my second husband's family. There were a few snapshots from my childhood, an old valentine, even my parents' wedding portrait, but when I worked my way down to the mat that should have held mine, it was empty; the girl I was and the dress I wore were gone.

I married my second husband in the living room of the house where we still live, and the only people in attendance were the bride, the groom, and the minister. The minister was, and is, a friend who earned a divinity degree from Duke before he moved to Greensboro, where he founded an underground paper and took an MFA. In the early '70s Jim had a street ministry on the hippie strip that adjoined our campus, and for years after he was asked to perform most of the town's alternative weddings. Ours was set for two o'clock, though at two we were all chatting awkwardly at the breakfast table, none of us willing to be the one to say, "It's time." At 2:05 the phone rang.

"Honey, I know you're busy getting married right now," my mother said, "but I thought you'd want to know Uncle Ernie had a stroke." It seemed as good a signal as any to begin.

The only witnesses were our dogs, one of whom humped Jim's leg throughout the ceremony. Too embarrassed to acknowledge the assault, he kept shaking his leg in an attempt to dislodge her. His voice quavered with the effort, and every word he read sounded like a sob. We were laughing so hard we could hardly get the job done. Though Jim had invited us to write our own vows, we hadn't bothered, and I can't remember what we promised, only that it stuck.

Jim has a lot of wedding stories, though I don't believe he's ever told ours. His favorite is about a biker whose pals lined up their Harleys and revved their engines in salute, though the wedding is just the preface, since the groom wiped out on his way to the honeymoon and a few days later Jim was back in the same meadow, eulogy in one hand, a Budweiser can full of ashes in the other. If you've seen *The Big Lebowski* you know the rest: bikers gun their engines in farewell, groom blows out of the can all over Jim's face. At least that's the way he tells it.

I had a friend whose trip from wedding to the obituary page was also far too brief. Like me, Marcy had been married before. She'd wanted children, but her husband, an up and coming assistant professor, felt they would hinder his career, and though my story lacks Jim's macabre humor, I'm sure he would appreciate the irony that the husband failed to get tenure after he left her for a student. I knew Marcy in the unhappy years while she was single, when she wanted nothing more than to marry again, which she did, rather suddenly, at forty. The wedding was scheduled for a garden, but it rained that day, and so she and her young groom said their vows in the parlor of the Ireland House, a nineteenth-century mansion restored for such occasions. They moved to Pennsylvania the day after the wedding, and though we kept in touch I saw her only once again, at her baby shower. It was a difficult birth, a C-section, and for months the doctors blamed the pain in her abdomen on that. She died of ovarian cancer just after her daughter's first birthday. Two months before she died the Ireland House burned down. For years I passed the site every day on my way home from the studio where I used to write, first the burnt out ruin, later the two stone arches that survived the demolition rising from the weedy grass behind a six-foot chain-link fence. It seemed to mock the whole idea of celebration.

It still saddens me to pass the Ireland House arches, though they could just as well serve as a reminder of how lucky I have been. I watched my child grow up. I had those young years when he was my best pal. I thought of those years last winter after his accident, when we spent so many hours together, he on his sofa, reading tide tables and napping, a little dopey from the pain pills, on his laptop or his cell phone making arrangements for an upcoming fishing school, while I read and walked his dog and did the dishes. Once he looked up and said he was sorry not to be better company, he just had so much work to do, and I said, "I have a book, I'm fine, actually I like this quiet time, it feels so companionable and cozy." "I like it too," he said.

He *survived* his accident; mine could have been so much worse. You never know when a careless driver, rowdy dog, or maverick cell might show up, and there's not much worry does to change the odds. Life is risky, and luck is always counted backwards. My son grew up, he moved away, and I miss him, but he's *here*.

He's here right now, though he'll be driving back to Wilmington this evening. It's Monday, Labor Day, the wedding festivities are over, and he has to get another issue of his paper out before he heads to Georgia to see the next friend married. But for the moment he's in the breakfast room downstairs, playing chess with another friend. It's something he misses at the coast, he tells me. For a while after this friend, Paul, and his girlfriend in Greensboro broke up, Paul considered buying a house in Wilmington, a move Max would have welcomed, not just for the regular chess games but the friend. In the last few years so many of his circle there have taken other jobs, moved away, or gotten married—already he is learning the way adult life narrows. But then Paul found another girlfriend in Greensboro and bought a house here instead.

Today he's come by to help load some lawn furniture and the gas grill I'm getting rid of into Max's truck. Last winter, in the brief time between his broken ankle and broken leg, when Max came home to work the Greensboro Boat and Fishing Expo, Paul helped him break down his booth and load the trailer. Paul was wearing Heelys that day, those rollie shoes with wheels inside the heels, and the first thing I said when I saw him was "I didn't know they made those in adult sizes." He laughed and told me that the first time he'd worn them he'd taken a bad spill, and instead of asking if he was okay, if she could help, the young woman who witnessed it said exactly the same thing. He cast a glance at my son's swollen leg and added, "I wouldn't recommend them for Max."

Once the chess match is over and they've got everything strapped down in Max's truck, they toss a football back and forth in the street while I stand at the window in my immobilizer, watching. "Don't forget your shoes," I say when Max comes upstairs to get his things. He gives me a thumbs up and picks up the hanger with his suit, putting the shoes on top of the laundry basket with the rest of his clothes. When he tries to return his father's tie, in unison we both say "keep it"—he'll be needing it in Georgia. His dad goes to his closet and comes back with another printed with crabs and barracudas. "Thanks!" Max says. He has a suit, a pair of dress shoes, and two ties now.

Later in the week I will find out my knee is broken and be locked into a brace—no more driving for six weeks at least, it's my turn for crutches and confinement, no sneaking out to buy baguettes or just to make sure the world's still there. My son knows all about such restrictions, and when we talk on the phone he understands how grateful I am to the two friends who visited that morning. While I was in Wilmington last winter the whole city seemed to drop in on him.

"You don't have as many friends coming by when you're laid up once you're older," I explain.

"I can see that," he says, then adds, "You don't have as many people stopping by once the novelty of a friend on the couch wears off either."

Sometimes I think of Marcy as the first friend of my adult life. She was the first friend of middle age, that time when you begin to lose so many companions of youth to distance or distractions or a season of divorce, and though I lost her too, for a time she was the promise that even as life seems to narrow it can also widen.

I was twenty-one years old the year I climbed to bed each night with a sense that my life was over. A newlywed, a girl whose whole life lay before her, even if she was too unhappy to discern it. Thirty-seven when I married again, in empire tea-length dress of ivory linen edged at the neckline with a narrow band of braid, bought at the Jeannette Maternity Outlet for something like twenty dollars, and I remember how I went to bed each night with an overwhelming sense of life instead of doom. Now I'm sixty-five, so much closer in my trip from the wedding pages to the obits, but even so I climb the stairs each night—or should say scootch, because the only way to climb with a broken knee is on your butt—with the sense that I am dancing.

MY DOG EATS THE PAST

———

BYE-BYE, CHILDHOOD. So long, my husband's early years. Sons, your achievements are confetti on the carpet. It's adios to first teeth, first words, and graduation photos. The dog is on a rampage. The past is no longer even history, the present is a clean-up job, all he's left us is that undocumented uncertainty we like to call the future.

It's my fault. For years after our last dogs died, those mongrel ingrates who refused to accept our newborn son, the one who bit him in the face when he chased her down in his walker at ten months, the same one my first husband and I named Lemon on the theory that everything else we'd owned had been one and the dog probably would be too, old Lemon, that one, and the other one, the sweet, dumb lab mix who snapped rabbits' necks with a single shake of her head and fearlessly faced down other dogs but stood in the corner trembling whenever our baby son was in the room, the one our older son, my stepson, called Blackie until she ran off and I walked the streets crying, "Blackie, Blackie, where are you?" and every black dog in Fayetteville, Arkansas came running—for years after those two dogs were gone my husband liked to say, "You can either have a new dog or a new husband, take your pick," and I would say, because what other response would anyone give to such an offer, "I'll get back to you."

Poor old Lemon spent the remaining three of her sixteen years in the yard, and Blackie, turned Blixie, trembled eight more years until she ran off again, this time to die. Our younger son didn't want a dog—why would he? And animal lovers though we are for a decade we did just fine without one, but then the son grew up and went away to college and one morning I went to the farmers' market for eggplant and came home with an eleven-week-old black Labrador puppy.

"Oh," my husband said when I rang the bell, and that was that. "The third son," he calls him, "sweet boy, the best dog that ever was dog," this dog that has suddenly, in his eighth year, decided to consume all evidence that we had a life before him.

We expected chewing from the pup, of course. One of my oldest cookbooks still bears the imprint of young Lemon's teeth. And though I don't recall Blixie chewing anything, I don't think we ever would have gotten that dog housebroken if my first husband hadn't decided to return Lemon. Lemon was half border collie; she knew how to keep other animals in line. But this one, little mister no-name for two days, our Mister Ollie, son of Serenity Sheila and Troubleshoot the Black Bear, descended of more Tarbabies than you can count, all the way back to the first St. John's dog of Newfoundland—because it's our past he's going after; his archives are intact—our sweet boy, the pupster, my pupperoni, best dog that ever was dog, teethed on bricks. He gnawed steel cables, swallowed rocks, paper clips, and staples. His first emergency visit to the vet came three days after we got him, when he scarfed a chicken bone off the street that lodged in his intestine, the second when he downed a quart of glazing compound the house painter left open on the deck. Our chairs have no rungs, we're on our third sofa and sixth quilt. As a pup he tore through the house beating beer cartons against the walls, he shredded wicker, stole the obligatory shoes, socks, and underwear, took bites of antique Persian rugs. No toy survived a day.

"Fill a Kong with fat-free cream cheese," the vet advised. "That's good for hours of chewing."

Within moments the cheese was gone and he was chowing down on little pieces of hard rubber. I bought him a bed; he ate it. I bought another; he ate it. I bought a third, a big, puffy raspberry-colored velvet pillow embroidered with a wish for *sweet dreams*. He peed on it. It was too fat to fit in the washing machine, so I threw it away, and whenever we left the house for the rest of his nearly three years of youthful indiscretions he slept on a plastic tray. Dogs love their crates, the experts swear. What we consider cages, they regard as doggie dens, sanctuaries, safe havens. Ollie hated his doggie den. His idea of sanctuary is a king-sized bed, preferably with lots of pillows and two masters he can crowd, air conditioning on full blast, along with the overhead fan. And if there's a tissue wadded on a nightstand, well, that's just breakfast in bed.

Labs are notorious chewers, but how would I have known? The lab before him—and there was one, Sid Vicious, the rescue puppy my son and his roommate adopted, a singularly unvicious soul my husband called Sidney the Zen Dog—was far too centered on inner peace for havoc. Labs are also known for digging, and for a few years our backyard looked like a Chicago street after a rough winter, but despite their highly developed instinct for destruction, they're the most popular breed in America. Labs are smart, they're goofy, they love everyone. Their enthusiasm is eternal; labs are happy dogs. When the dog was first domesticated some fifteen thousand years ago, the evolutionary process privileged the qualities of the pup over those of the mature gray wolf from which all dogs, great Danes and Chihuahuas alike, are descended: the sociability, the shorter nose, larger head and eyes, the softer coat and floppy ears, a phenomenon scientists call paedomorphic selection. And labs, with their big block heads and silk-purse ears (there is nothing softer or smoother or more soothing to the touch than a Labrador's ear), their love of games, their rowdy energy and boundless affections, are a paedomorphic triumph.

One especially relentless night not long after Ollie arrived, Mike sat with his head in his hands at the breakfast room table and moaned, "I'm too old for this," and I had to promise that if we could just get through the manic puppy stage, he would be a great dog, though I had no confidence myself. Still, even for lab owners, there comes a day when you believe your unmentionables, your shoes and socks and household furnishings are safe, when you can give the detested crate, your doggie den, away. Ollie was over two and a half when he was liberated, and for five years—half a decade—we foolishly imagined that we too were home free.

———

FIRST TO GO WAS my childhood photograph album, left on the floor of my study because I was using it to check a date for an essay I was writing. My study is a messy place, and the floor around my desk was heaped with folders spilling notes. Still, stumbling into the room without my glasses on the morning after the crime, I was mystified by the black crumbs on the carpet. Not until I saw the album did I realize that sometime in the night Ollie must have snuck from our bed into my workroom, because there it was, the evidence, the album that pictured me from birth through high school, its binding chewed down through the cardboard, the ravaged black pages and mangled old black and white Kodaks with their deckled edges and impossibly remote dates still wet with saliva.

I would like to say that I was shocked, and in fact I was, though I can't say we weren't warned. Some months before Ollie had gnawed a book Mike left on the sofa, not the fifty-cent paperback from the thrift store smelling of mildew and dust but the handsome hardback signed to me by the author/friend. We were horrified—our house is full of books—though we joked about the title. Of course he ate the book. It was called *Winter's Bone*.

And it's true that all along there had been aberrations—the occasional potholder found damp and ragged on the foyer rug (but those are always so stained, so saturated with grease and well-aged juices, really, what dog could be expected to resist?), the pilfered steak knives and shredded Ziplocs, their contents just a smear of memory on the plastic, and yes, two Thanksgivings ago Ollie and my son's lab, Clyde, ate the entire pumpkin pie off the kitchen counter, but we blamed Clyde, and besides that same year a friend's very well-behaved dog ate the family turkey. "What are you so upset for? It's not like anyone was going to eat the pie," my son said by way of comfort, which did not make me feel better, though he did have a point: who has room for dessert after Thanksgiving dinner, unless the dog eats the turkey too? So, yes, aberrations—but you see, they all had to do with food.

Next was my husband's *Log of Life*, the tall white clothbound baby book, far more substantial a meal than my slender edition with its peeling pink laminated cover, though it too would go within the month. "You need to keep your study door closed," Mike had scolded when I showed him my album, but he was much too distressed about his *Log* for me to say the same. It was the pattern that was so troubling, more than the loss of the object itself. And even if I had been willing to throw Mike's admonition back at him, there was nothing I could say. We live in an old house; his study door is one of several that do not latch. Nor had he left the baby book out. It and the graduation portrait of my stepson that was apparently next on Ollie's list had been neatly tucked into the back shelf on the far side of his desk. Sweet boy would have had to work his way through a jumble of books, clothes, and papers to find what he was after.

So we vowed to keep our mementoes out of reach, but labs are big dogs, their reach is high, and the truth is the past is heavy. Only the lowest shelves will bear its weight.

———

BUT WHAT DOES THE PAST mean to a dog? Dogs take no pleasure in reviewing yesterday's walk; they want today's. Ollie wants his breakfast, his dinner, his Science Diet Chicken Lite treats, his spoonful of peanut butter, his romp in the woods, he wants his sweet spot, his pat-down, he wants that we should throw him balls the way we used to, before he tore his ACL, before he was diagnosed with dysplasia, so what if he limps, he wants to run and spin triple axels as he leaps to pluck the ball from the air, what's the matter with us anyway?

He has none of the yellowing memorabilia we humans tend to amass, though he's not without records, the pedigree chart, the registration papers we never bothered to send in, the overflowing red file folder of vet bills, and receipts, the service order for the invisible fence, his insurance policy and contact number for his microchip, the brochures for pet resorts and puppy playschools, not to mention all the pictures I've taken of him—Ollie on the sofa, Ollie at the park, Ollie on the porch, Ollie in the surf, Ollie, Ollie, Ollie. On videotape he still bounds, vaults, and catches. But I'm the one who saved these things; the past is no museum to him, not a collection of souvenirs but a living thing coded into his body. It's in his DNA, not just his own history, but that of all his forebears, and not just the Tarbabies, Serenity Sheilas, and Black Bears hunkered on the branches of his family tree, but all the dogs that came before them, back to the first St. John's dog exported from Newfoundland to England, back even further, some fifteen thousand years, to the moment the first hunter-gatherer threw the wolf a bone.

That was the beginning of civilization as we know it. The dog was the first domesticated animal; it was the dog who made agriculture possible, who allowed man to settle down and start collecting. It may be a footnote on the prehistoric past to us, but the dog remembers, remembers the beneficence of the hand that delivered the tibia with its dripping strings of meat, remembers the taste of the wet feathers on the first duck the wolf did not eat himself but because the man had shown him kindness delivered instead to the hunter destined to become his master.

He can't tell you the date, but neither can the scientists, who speculate that the vast number of specialized breeds suggests it may have been far longer ago than the fossil evidence shows. Once it was thought that the domestication of the dog took place in China; more recent evidence argues for the Middle East, where the first dog to be buried with his master was interred twelve thousand years ago. Fast forward to 2011, when the state of New York announced that its animal cemeteries would no longer accept the cremains of people who want to spend eternity with their pets, a decision that upset a lot of pet lovers—after all, twelve thousand years makes for a pretty

well-established tradition. I thought of Peggy Guggenheim in
the garden wall in Venice with her "babies." On Ocracoke Island
the wealthy eccentric Sam Jones is interred beside his horse. But
mostly I thought of Joe, my husband's first Hospice patient. His
beloved Shetland sheepdog had only one tooth and was so long
in that Mike feared that the dog would die before the master,
who had been a jazz drummer, lived the smoky club life, and was
paying the price with COPD. The dog survived him by a day.
According to the vet Shelly the Sheltie had willed himself to
last until his master left him. Their ashes were buried together
in Joe's snare drum. I love that story, though, frankly, it's never
occurred to me that I might want to snooze through an afterlife
with Ollie. He hogs the bed.

It's a long and complicated route from the untamed wolf to
him, and no one yet has fully mapped it, though for more than
fifty years researchers at the Institute of Cytology and Genetics
in Siberia have been breeding foxes with the goal of re-creating
the evolution of wolf into dog in order to decode the mystery of
domestication. Paedomorphic selection is not unique to dogs.
To some extent it can be seen in a number of species, even fish,
though not all animals can be domesticated, and the why of that
is one of the many secrets that remain unknown. Still it's clear
that the process is genetic. The speed with which the Siberian
researchers have succeeded is astonishing. Only nine generations in, a scant decade, changes in the foxes were no longer just
behavioral. Ears no longer stood up soon after birth, and the
first kits with spotted coats were born. A few more generations
and their bone structure began to change. Half a century later
there are forty genes worth of difference between their descen-
dents and the control group of wild foxes. Nearly any animal
can be tamed if the process begins early enough, but taming and
domestication are not the same thing, nor would the domestication of the dog have been as purposeful or controlled a procedure

as the fox experiment. Virtually everyone who studies such things agrees: the dog was not just willing, it was eager.

———

MORE THAN ANY OTHER animal, dogs are cherished for their loyalty, the unconditional nature of their love. But loyalty is more than love; it requires memory. Yet conventional wisdom maintains that dogs have no memory, no long-term memory, that is, and a short-term one so brief that no impression lasts beyond five minutes. All the training books tell us so as they warn us not to punish the puppy for peeing in the house or devouring a shoe unless we catch him in the act, because he won't make the connection between the crime and our hard words. But that's not because a dog lacks memory; it's because a dog's memory is associative. So is mine. I may be able to grasp abstract concepts and memorize facts that Ollie can't—that is, as far as we can know what he grasps—but the dates I learned for the high school history test are gone. I can summon the multiplication table because I use it. I know your name because I see you. Without all those prompts from the past—the baby books, the photographs, the ticket stubs, programs, day books, and albums, all those things Ollie seems bent upon destroying—how long do I expect memory to last? Since I began writing nonfiction, my old calendars and albums have become invaluable references. I look up one thing I remember and pick up clues to twenty I forgot.

Those are the clues I tend to privilege—a word here, a picture there. But dogs neither perceive the world nor remember the same way. Sight is not their primary sense, which is why they do so well with so little adjustment when they go blind. Their memory is in their ears and in their nose. Dogs *listen*, and their hearing is acute. Not only do they perceive frequencies we can't, they change the position of their outer ears in order to magnify and focus. Even after an absence of many years a dog can identify familiar voices. Ten months after I left Lemon with my first husband and went off to graduate school, she recognized the sound of our old Renault as I turned the corner toward home, and all the way down the street I watched her twitch and yelp with joy in anticipation of my arrival.

It was that memory for sound that reunited Sid and Ollie. For a while when Ollie was a pup, Sidney the Zen Dog spent occasional weekends at our house. When we went to Italy the spring after we got him, Ollie spent three weeks with Max. Though Sid no longer shared Max's house, he and his official owner, Stephen, visited nearly every day. The two labs were soul brothers, romping, wrestling, despite Sid's Buddhist nature flying through the house. But then Stephen moved to New York, I bought Clyde for Max, and Ollie and Clyde took up where Ollie and Sid left off—rugs up the wall, chairs overturned, no lamp left standing. Clyde's a soul brother too. Something like four or five years had passed since Ollie had last seen Sid when a special bark sounded from the far side of a local park where Mike was walking Ollie, that is, to Mike's ear a bark like any other but special to Ollie, whose ears pricked and nose quivered as he yelped and took off, dragging Mike until he reached his goal, five hundred wooded feet away, a small black lab with a wave down the back of his coat, Ollie's first and original soul brother, Sid Vicious, who was visiting Stephen's parents in Greensboro. The dogs were ecstatic.

But as keen as a dog's retention for sound may be, it is the nose where the collective unconsciousness of the species resides. Every walk is an investigation into the past, from the sandwich wrapper dropped last month to the last dog to pee on the lamppost at the corner—and the one before that and the one before that. Scent is a dog's calendar, and though they could just as well squat as they did when they were puppies, male dogs lift their legs to pee in order to aim their scent as high as they can get it so that the next dog to come along will sniff and think, *Man, I do not want to mess with him, that is one big mother.* The first time I saw Ollie lift his leg he was squatting. His left hind paw rose no more than an inch off the ground, and he turned his head to check it out. If a dog can be said to frown, he frowned. *What is that all about?* At six months his body remembered something he had not yet learned. As the owner of a local kennel puts it, "We get email; they get pee mail." We shake hands; they sniff each other's butts.

You would think that around five million sense receptors, the number humans have, would be more than anyone could need to decipher any odor until you consider that dogs possess in the neighborhood of two hundred twenty million. The area of the nose containing our equipment for the job is no bigger than a postage stamp, but if that spongy, scrolled place inside a dog's nose were unfolded it would be as large as a diploma. Proportionately a dog's brain is only half the size of ours, but the percentage of that brain devoted to the analysis of smells is forty times larger. No wonder a dog can detect scents with a concentration one hundred million times lower than you or I can. Observe the way the slits that curve up from a dog's nostrils open to let more air reach the receptors at the back of the snout. With a single sniff he can detect virtually any volatile organic compound, which is to say any compound that contains molecules capable of becoming airborne. But once is seldom enough, and fortunately for him, a pocket in his nasal cavity allows him to collect enough to parse the scent. I hear the primitive sound that cavity makes whenever Ollie sniffs with particular concentration. There is a hollow reverberation inside his nose like a drum, a rhythmic throb that approximates the most elemental sound we know, the heartbeat.

That heartbeat is the sound of a dog thinking, and it is nearly impossible to get Ollie to move on until he's satisfied that he has correctly identified whatever it is he smells and that archetypal drumming stops.

It was an acute sense of smell that not only allowed the first mammals, small shrew-like creatures, to sniff out food at night and avoid being eaten by the dinosaurs but also drove an explosive growth in the size of mammals' brains and the development of the neocortex, the outer layer of the cerebral hemispheres unique to mammals that is involved in higher functions. That sense of smell was the bedrock of their intelligence. We're here because the most ancient creatures of our kind could sniff out safety. And it is the dog's superior capacity for analyzing odors that makes him the most intelligent of all domesticated animals.

A dog can smell a single drop of blood in fifty-five gallons of water and a teaspoon of sugar in a million. He can smell one milligram of butyric acid, a natural component of human body odor, in 100,000,000 cubic meters of air. He can smell your moods. Law enforcement agencies and rescue operations make extensive use of labs, German shepherds, and Belgian malinois because of those breeds' particular skills at detecting explosives, illegal substances, and human beings, even from considerable distances. As we know, they track criminals and missing people. The eighty-member Navy SEAL team that took out Osama bin Laden included a dog, who was strapped to one of the SEALs as they were lowered from the helicopter. Dogs who searched for human remains in the aftermath of the World Trade Center attack had to be rotated and retired because the job was so depressing. There are 2700 dogs on active duty in the American military, and more than eight hundred canine teams work with the U.S. Department of Homeland Security. Dogs can sniff out cancer, impending seizures, bedbug infestations, agricultural contraband, invasive weeds in fields, allowing them to be eradicated before they take hold, cows in heat for the purpose of artificial insemination, and the chemical components of pirated DVDs.

Which brings me to the question at hand: Why is our lab, who has been groomed for none of those useful tasks, who spends a large part of each day sleeping on the sofa and would prefer to roll in the weeds or eat the DVDs, who is surely smart enough to have been trained as an assist dog, but has been taught only not to pee or poop in the house, to come when called, to sit on command, though sometimes he prefers to think that one over, to wait until given permission when the dinner bowl is set down, and not to jump on guests, though he does so anyway, why is our pupster, Oshti, Ols, Sweezil, Oshtcrenko, the Ollinator, my pooch pie, bearer of that noble Labrador profile and all those potential skills, our sweet boy whose only job is to serve as our third son, devouring all the irreplaceable images and words that are the keys to the vault we call our past? Why the albums, why the pictures, why the hardbound book and not the folder full of notes?

Labs are born to be hunters or retrievers, but not both. Hunters wander; retrievers fetch. Ollie is a retriever. Chasing balls was the most cherished part of his day. Outside he played the field; indoors he played stair ball; while I was fixing dinner we rolled the spheroid back and forth along the kitchen floor. He and Mike invented a game called Lolo, a game of concentration in which a Kong toy was placed between them on a rug and spun; each tried to outwit the other for the pounce, but they had to quit when Ollie got so good at anticipating Mike's every strategy that there was no longer any sport. He was performing a spectacular catch when he tore his ACL and the X-ray discovered his dysplasia. His glory days are over. And he misses them.

There is also the matter of the glue. I was thinking along the lines of old Dobbin and the glue factory when I began my research, but the glue's not made of hooves—it's fish, fish oil

used in bookbinding and the adhesives in albums. A lab will
eat almost anything, including the TV remote, and mine is not
the only one rooting through the mulch for a favored delicacy,
lured by the smell his peerless nose can't miss, the ambrosia of
tuna in that exquisite doggie treat, the cat turd.

It's not our past he's going after; it's the glue that holds it
together.

———

BUT WHAT DOES the past mean to us?

To my mother it's the endless loop of the childhood she
narrates for me every time I see her, the one she practices
remembering by way of insisting she'd like to forget. She's a
sentimental woman, so bound to her particular past that for
her bad memories are better than none. She has no memory
of her mother, who died when she was seven. Perhaps that's
why she obsesses over those things she wants to pass on to me.
Don't I want my baby shoes? Surely I need the leaf collection
I made for ninth-grade science, a pair of coat hooks from my
grade school, my first bank, my band medals, a stained slip
once worn by my aunt Eleanor, a plastic baggie full of my hair,
another full of hers, and what about her dishes, service for
twelve, not to mention the snack tables she tiled and grouted
to match with dye she made from coffee, who's going to take
these things, what will happen to them if I don't? "Mom," I say,
"Where would I put the stuff?" But how will I remember what
color my hair used to be, what color hers was, how clever she
is, what if I forget her?

It's mothers who are the usual keepers of the baby books
and family albums. But if they are the authors of our early
past, who is its audience? Certainly I was not a good audience for mine. There was nothing in my baby book that could
have triggered memory, good or bad—it was prehistory to me,

a time before memory began. So far Ollie has left my son's
intact, though I doubt Max will claim it. His grandmother's
attachment to yesteryear did not pass down to him. He keeps
no pictures, saves nothing. Like Clyde, like Ollie, he's a creature of the moment. And though I was groomed for sentiment
by my mother—witness all those shelves of albums just waiting for Ollie to dispatch—I discover I don't care about those
things nearly as much as I thought. The family videotapes go
unwatched, the albums gather dust. The past is gone; it's the
present we fear losing, and so, shutterbug that I am, I record
it, though in doing so, I see now, I'm not capturing the present
but documenting the moment when the very act of recording
turns the present into past.

There's too much of it. The shelves are full, the file drawers
overflowing, stuffed with manuscripts, records, proof sheets,
slides, and old correspondence. *There's no more room*, no room
for more pictures, no room for those trinkets that remind
me where I've been—the Venetian glass, the Tuscan pottery,
linens from Provence, Greek icons and silver jewelry, London's
Wedgwood and Spode, the petrified wood, volcanic rocks,
seashells, magnets, and coffee mugs. Enough's enough. The
calendars that are so important to my writing take up one full
drawer. I'll have to empty a new one come January. "I've lived
long enough," my father said at eighty, just before he killed
himself. I have not. There's too much I want to do, and the
morning air is so fresh, the light so lovely. But it's the present
that I crave. I've reached the age where the tangible past is
too bulky to drag behind me. Even my son won't take the old
editions of *The Fisherman's Post* with his name on the masthead,
his byline and pictures inside. I have his baby teeth—who
wants them? What's to be done with our teaching awards and
literary prizes? Let cyberspace keep my correspondence. It's
time to say farewell to the historical detritus of our lives—*auf*

Wiedersehen, arrivederci, au revoir, yasou, aloha, shalom. After all, even the books I've written will one day end up at the Salvation Army thrift shop.

But until they do, for now, we've settled on distraction. Each night Ollie gets a Nylabone, the big one, to chew for an hour. Although he tires of it in fifteen minutes, he looks forward to it every night. Supposedly they're indestructible, but he wears them down to nubs pretty quickly. I buy them in bulk.

———

AND WHAT OF THE PRESENT, so soon to turn into past? Once those other dogs, Lemon and Blixie, were there beside me. It was their fur I smelled, their warm bellies I rubbed, their glad whimpers sounding in my ears. Then it was the baby who fit so snugly between wrist and elbow, whose heat I pressed against my skin, whose *da*'s and *ga*'s, those first gleeful stabs at words, delighted my ears, but whose precise baby smell I can no longer reconstruct, for that dear infant body has disappeared into the man's. No matter how much I remember, the past can never again, not through any of its clues, be the sensory, palpable now.

And in that lush and tactile now it's Ollie who is here, Ollie who keeps company with me afternoons on the screened porch while I read, and when I look up to admire him on the wicker loveseat that he's claimed I sometimes think that I can't bear it: that handsome profile with its noble jowl and perfect stop, the intelligent brown eyes, the rich calligraphy of his nose and the follicles where his whiskers grow, black velvet dots on black velvet, the soft loop of skin at the back of his mouth like a teardrop laid sideways, the silk pennants of his ears and deep luster of his coat and beneath his paws the thick black tufts of hair growing between the sturdy charcoal-colored pads like moss among the rocks in a swiftly running river. He's a gorgeous creature; no picture does him justice. But what breaks my heart is not the beauty of his visage, but the beauty of his attention, the way his eyes arch up and triangulate whenever he hears something he wants to consider, the way his ears shift as his nose twitches and his whiskers quiver. I can't read it, but I see his mind at work. Then the sound that I can't hear subsides, his chin drops to his paws, his eyes half close, though when I touch my hand to the sun-warmed fur along his side, he tips his muzzle up. He wants the sweet spot, and as I rub his muscled throat, he hooks a paw around my arm to hold me, and I think that I might cry because the single lesson all those tokens from the past have to teach us is that loss is the only certainty the future offers, the one terrible sure thing. But we are here, and it is now. He licks my face, and I am laughing even as my heart beats out its impossible command. *Ollie, stay.*

BUZZARDS

———

THEY WOOF. Though I have photographed them before, I have never heard them speak, for they are mostly silent birds. Lacking a syrinx, the avian equivalent of the human larynx, they are incapable of song. According to field guides the only sounds they make are grunts and hisses, though the Hawk Conservancy in the United Kingdom reports that adults may utter a croaking coo and young black vultures, when annoyed, emit a kind of immature snarl. But to hear any of these sounds, you must be quite close. And I am quite close. Crouched over an unextended tripod at the edge of an empty parking lot in the Everglades, I am in the middle of a flock of black vultures,

a vortex, maypole for this uneasy circle dance in which they
weave and run at one another, raising their ragged wings and
thrusting their gnarly gray heads. I would not call the sound
they make a grunt or a hiss, nor croaking coo, nor snarl; it is
more a low, embryonic woofing, a sound I know from my dog,
who is also a black creature, not a bark or growl, not the voice
itself, but the anticipation of one reverberating deep inside
his throat. And though I keep shooting as they lurch at one
another and dip their heads to peck at bottle caps and flattened
pieces of tin, they creep me out. I have had the same sensation
while snorkeling, an exhilaration in the magic of a world not
mine that manifests itself in the same nauseous thrill of nerve
as my dread. Buzzards. Carrion crows, Jim Crow, Charleston
eagle. *Coragyps atratus.* From the Greek *korax*, meaning "raven"
and *gyps*, meaning "vulture," Latin *atratus*, "clothed in black,
as in mourning." The Grim Reaper's hooded cloak, wing-like
sleeves, and skeletal feet all come to us as a personification
of the black vulture; Death's trademark scythe is the color
and shape of the flight feathers, the long white primaries the
bird displays as he hunches and spreads his wings. The Latin
vulturus means "tearer." Give voice to the word and you cannot
distinguish it from terror.

———

TO PHOTOGRAPH BIRDS requires a great deal of equipment.
I paid for most of mine—the carbon steel tripod and expensive
ball head, the camera bodies, lenses, flash, filter, reflectors, and
remote—with money I inherited from my father. He would
not have approved. He disapproved of most things. Though
he could rage, he was a mostly silent man who had no respect
for impractical pursuits. He was not a bad man, though he was
difficult, excitable, hard on others, obsessed with money. The
first time I visited the Everglades he tried to talk me out of

it—it was too far, he said, there was nothing there; instead he recommended that I visit Silver Springs, a nature theme park boasting glass-bottom boat tours and a narrated Jeep safari. He wasn't much for nature in the wild. He liked control. He was afraid of the unknown, not of death, but of life, which had too many variables. It was the unpredictable and irritating otherness of others that frightened him most.

What frightens me is the otherness of vultures. I am wondering whether they will tear at my flesh, raise their wings, and run at me. I should know, but I don't.

To photograph a wild creature, you must learn its habits.

———

THE BIBLE DOES NOT differentiate between birds of prey and vultures, which are rarely predators, living instead as scavengers, consumers of carrion. One might even call them connoisseurs, for they prefer their meat fresh and the turkey vulture favors the flesh of herbivores over that of carnivores. According to the Carolina Raptor Center, in captivity they won't eat possum, which is greasy, but happily chow down on rats. The black also feasts on fruit, though it has an unfortunate taste for turtle hatchlings, unlike the palm nut vulture of Africa, a vegetarian that is surely the strangest of the twenty-three species that populate the world. But in Biblical wisdom both predator and scavenger are unclean and hateful birds; if raptors are God's creatures, according to the Book of Leviticus, they are also an abomination: "And these are they which ye shall have in abomination among the fowls…the eagle, and the ossifrage, and the osprey, and the vulture…." Ossifrage, from the Latin *ossifraga*, meaning bone-breaker, is an archaic name for the bearded vulture, an Old World species once plentiful in the Alps, Himalayas, and Pyrenees, the only vulture to consume bone as the primary part of its diet. Ornithologists no longer sanction use of the bird's other names, lamb vulture and *lammergeyer*, since it is incapable of killing lambs, let alone babies, despite the myths that have led to its near extinction. While some vultures prey on insects and small amphibians and the black will steal young herons from the nest, they rarely attack live mammals. More than once I have come out my back door to discover a puff of feathers light as dandelion fluff beneath the azaleas, signature of a hawk that has raided the feeder; thrice I have been startled by the sight of a great blue heron advancing across my small city yard toward the pond. Only recently scientists have confirmed that our ancestors, the ape men, were not killed off by ferocious saber-toothed tigers but by eagles, which hunt primates larger than themselves by swooping down and piercing their skulls with their strong back talons. These are predators. "I hate vultures because they only frighten humans," says Mrs. MacKinnon in the Book of Animals, Plants, Trees, Birds, Bugs, and Flowers that informs Craig Nova's novel *The Good Son*. The titmice and chickadees, the thrashers and towhees, chipmunks, squirrels, fantails, koi, and Labrador retriever who share the space of my garden do not fear the vulture.

When Charles Darwin observed the "carrion-feeding hawks" of Uruguay in the summer of 1832, he lamented that although their structure placed them among the eagles, they ill became such a rank. Though Darwin was a self-taught observer rather than a trained scientist, even the most learned scientists of the time mistakenly believed that the New World vultures were related to the eagles. While the Old World vultures that inhabit Africa, Asia, and parts of Europe, did descend from the birds of prey classified as Falconiformes, the seven species that inhabit the Americas are classified as Ciconiiformes, related not to hawks but to storks. The similarities in appearance—the wattled necks, small naked heads, hooked beaks, weak though fearsome-looking talons, shaggy feathers, and pronounced hunch—are the result of convergent evolution, like but independent physical adaptations.

Yet so inevitable is the vulture's association with death and so staunch our cultural will to deny it, that we persist in the Biblical view of the vulture even as we tend to perceive those raptors from which the Old World vultures descended, the hawks and eagles, as Darwin did: creatures of grace, nobility, and strength, equated with freedom instead of death. Darwin called the turkey buzzard a "disgusting bird" whose bald scarlet head is "formed to wallow in putridity." He was right about the formation of the head—bacteria die on the bare skin of the face, just as the bird's practice of defecating on its legs kills bacteria. Their habits may seem repulsive, but in fact vultures are among the cleanest of creatures. Adult condors wipe their heads and necks on grass or sand after feeding; while other carrion eaters spread disease, the acids in the vulture's digestive system are so strong they destroy anthrax, botulin, cholera, and hanta-virus—the birds can consume the most toxic corpses without passing the germs along.

In *The Vulture,* novelist Catherine Heath describes a pet vulture that preys on its master's thoroughbred dogs as "a huddle of old rags thrown over a naked body, whose stringy neck and red head stuck out at the top as if surveying a hostile world from a safe shelter." The buzzards that perch on the light posts of Arrow Catcher, Mississippi in Lewis Nordan's *Wolf Whistle* sit "with hunched shoulders and wattled necks like sad old men in dark coats," and Ernest Hemingway calls them "huge, filthy birds sunk in hunched feathers." The villainous protagonist of "The Tell-Tale Heart" kills not out of passion or greed, but because his victim has the eye of a vulture. Pablo Neruda speaks not of the vulture's appearance but his black habits. It is these habits that have made "vultures" into a favorite epithet for the media. We use it for politicians, lawyers, ambulance chasers, talk-show audiences, corporations, and nosy neighbors. Photographers are often called vultures. So are writers.

———

WHEN MY FATHER DIED, his companion of nearly twenty years told me, "Be sure to take your stories." I found the books I'd signed to both of them at the back of his closet. Though there were a few books on their living room shelves, mine had never been among them. My father was ashamed of my writing. I know because he said as much to my mother, though they were already divorced. Otherwise I would not have known he read them, for he never mentioned them to me. He was ashamed not just of the writing itself but of the fact that I wrote. He didn't see the point. He kept a log of his gas mileage, but he never kept a journal. Skilled at repair, he gave to objects the kind of attention he could not deliver to people; yet I have no recollection of his hands, no memory of the texture of his skin or shape of his nails. He had beautiful handwriting, but no use for words.

———

VULTURES ARE BIG BIRDS. The largest bird that ever existed was a vulture of the Pleistocene epoch with a wingspan of sixteen to seventeen feet. Weighing up to thirty-three pounds, with a ten and a half foot wingspan that dwarfs a grand piano, the Andean condor is still the largest and heaviest bird that flies; climbers compare the sound of the wind rushing through its feathers to that of a jet plane. The largest of the Old World species, the Himalayan griffon, is only slightly smaller. Wingtip to wingtip the turkey vulture measures seventy-nine inches and is larger than the American black, which has the shortest wingspan of all, a mere fifty-four inches. But to crouch in the shadow of the black's scythe-tipped wings and feel the sweep of their breath as they open is to lose all sense of inches. This smallest emissary of death has an embrace of four and a half feet. When they are even partially unfolded, the bird must hunch to keep its wings from dragging on the ground.

———

IN YOUTH, MY FATHER was a handsome man, tall and broad-shouldered. On the street people sometimes mistook him for the rising film star John Wayne, though by the time I was old enough to remember he was already balding, no longer auburn but gray, with the same harried look on his face of other middle-aged men who worked whatever jobs they could find to pay the mortgage and feed their families. Perhaps they had wanted children; my father never did. He would have rather sailed on the tankers he loaded before punching a clock and then driving home. I don't think his work gave him pleasure, nor do I think he thought it should. For him pleasure was a sign of weak character.

———

ON THE GROUND A GROUP of vultures is called a venue, but a group circling in the air is a kettle, as if they are swirling in a clear cauldron, a school of black fish swimming in a soup of pure air. Ungainly on the ground with their small heads, oversized wings, and heavy bodies, a gait that is at once a lurch and a run, vultures are astonishingly graceful in flight, a glide "in God's fingerprint," according to George Garrett. Darwin marveled at the sight of condors soaring in high, graceful circles. Even the turkey buzzard he found so abhorrent is transformed on the wing "by its lofty, soaring and most elegant flight;" Lewis Nordan's vultures sail "like hopeful prayers."

Who has not watched them wheel overhead? Floating high
above the landfills that punctuate the flatness of the interstate
along the east coast of Florida, they undulate like kites teth-
ered to the earth by invisible strings. In the mountains I thrill
to discover how close I am to heaven by the arc of a turkey
vulture swooping below. I am too dazzled by the wideness of
the sky to connect the dots of the constellations, and I forget
the names of all but the most basic forms of clouds; though
I know the field markings of many birds, I cannot tell a vireo
from a shrike in the air; but even at a distance far too great to
note the shorter tail of the black or difference in coloration on
the underside of the wings, I can easily distinguish between
black and turkey vultures in flight. The turkey rarely beats its
wings, holding them raised in a dihedral as it tilts from side to
side, rocking as if buoyed by a gentle sea; the black holds its
wings flat, beats more often, and does not tilt. Lacking a sense
of smell, it flies higher than the turkey, whose olfactory sense
is so keen engineers look for circling turkey vultures to locate
gas leaks and NASA used them to find remains of the ill-fated
crew of the space shuttle Columbia. The magnifying center
of the black vulture's eye is so powerful it can locate food by
sight from more than a mile above, though it often follows the
turkey to a corpse. Indians of the South American highlands
roast and consume condors' eyes in the belief that their own
eyesight will be sharpened.

In the tropics the king vulture too flies higher than the
turkey; in the dense rainforest both it and the black must
depend upon the *Cathartes*, the turkeys and yellow-heads, to
locate carrion by smell. With its gaudy orange, red, yellow,
purple, and black wattled head, the king is the most flamboyant; in flight its white back and long ebony-tipped wings are
spectacular. Rounding a curve of road in the Alajuela Province
of Costa Rica one Christmas, our van flushed a king vulture

from his roost on the living fence, and I gasped as he spread his wings and slowly swept across the cassava field to the forest canopy beyond, so stunned by the sight that he was gone before I remembered the camera beside me on the seat.

Vultures soar. Unlike most birds, whose breast muscles power the beating of the wings, creating lift and propulsion, a vulture simply opens its wings to the air currents that lift and keep it aloft. Once in a storm so torrential I pulled to the side of the interstate, I watched a small bird flying in place, flapping its wings frenetically against the wind, which finally blew it backward, as if it were no more than a bit of ash. The vulture's flight is so beautiful because it appears effortless. And in fact it nearly is, for a vulture uses scarcely more energy to fly than it would in standing still. It's not surprising that the Wright brothers should have designed their first plane with the curved wingtips of the turkey vulture in mind. According to Michael Alford Andrews, Andean condors spread their wingtip primaries "like fingers feeling for life as they turn." David Houston explains that once a vulture has gained altitude by circling inside a thermal, it can "glide away into still air, where it will slowly lose altitude" until it nears the ground, finds another thermal, and climbs again. They travel at remarkably high altitudes, as great as 15,000 feet for the vultures of Africa and the Andean condor; Houston reports a Ruppell's griffon alleged to have collided with a commercial aircraft at 37,000 feet. Imagine the alarm of passengers looking out a plane's window to see a vulture cruising just off the wing like a seagull following a boat's wake.

———

IT IS SAID THAT VULTURES circled above Romulus and Remus. Over and over they appear in literature and film as a dark omen. In Alain Robbe-Grillet's *Jealousy* the vulture pictured atop a mast on a calendar seems to confirm in the husband's mind his wife's infidelity. The hero of Ernest Hemingway's "The Snows of Kilimanjaro" knows that he is going to die when the buzzards move in, three "squatting obscenely" on the ground while a dozen swirl overhead "making quick-moving shadows." In Zora Neale Hurston's *Their Eyes Were Watching God* a thousand buzzards precede the deadly hurricane. In William Faulkner's *As I Lay Dying*, it is the sight of vultures in the distance that tell Darl his mother has died. And whenever we see them in a cartoon or Hollywood western, we know another outlaw is expiring just over the next hill.

———

MY FATHER DIED shortly after noon. He shot himself in the treeless backyard of the Florida house he shared with his companion, which backed on the open fairway of the community golf course, though he did not play. She had gone to the beauty parlor. When she returned a few hours later, she went through the house calling his name. She saw him through the window. I don't know if she stepped outside. In any case I'm sure she wouldn't have looked up.

———

THOUGH FROM THE VULTURE'S point of view it would hardly seem to matter which side prevails, many nations have used vultures as symbols of victory. Wayne Grady's eclectic and fascinating *Vulture: Nature's Ghastly Gourmet* lists several ancient monuments decorated with gruesome depictions of vultures devouring or hovering over the slain enemy. Grady also recalls Samuel Johnson's fable "The Vulture," in which a female is overheard instructing her young in the arts of a vulture's life—the easiest way to find food, she tells them, is to look for the place where enemies wage war. In the first scene of *Patton*, which opens with the image of an African white-backed vulture sitting on the mountain above the film's title, soldiers shoot two vultures to keep them from the battle-field corpses, denying them the cherished memories of Lewis Nordan's ancient Mississippi buzzards, who endure the lean twentieth century of roadkill by feasting on their recollection of "the glorious Festival of Dead Rebels."

But as the turkey vulture has extended its range north-ward, some see the bird not as the harbinger of death but the harbinger of spring. Bruce Ehresman, a biologist with the Iowa Department of Natural Resources, calls turkey vultures "much more reliable than robins," and Scott Weidensaul, whose observations contest the notion that turkey vultures are nonmigratory, maintains that they are the real sign of spring in the central Appalachians, reappearing "most often around the first week of February," followed by common grackles, then the red-winged blackbirds, until finally the robin returns at the end of February or early March, though only if the snow has melted. Here, on the Piedmont Plateau of North Carolina, I see no such sign, and so I wait for the Bradford pears and poke around the ivy for crocus.

———

MY FATHER WAS FROM WISCONSIN. He grew tired of waiting for spring, and when he retired he moved to Florida. He might have moved to El Paso, but he didn't like the radio station. In Florida, he reported proudly, it was summer nearly all year round, which is why the black vulture, which does not tolerate cooler temperatures as well as the turkey, is so common there. Vultures used to drink from the bucket beneath his downspout.

———

I HAVE OFTEN OBSERVED black vultures at Florida's Myakka River State Park. There they flock in great numbers, trolling the air above the lake, roosting on railings and roofs as if they are basking—and perhaps they are—the russet winter afternoon sun warming their dull black feathers and lending a subtle lavender to the wrinkled gray skin of their heads. One year when they seemed particularly active, I spotted half a dozen standing on a car parked beside the lake, where they appeared to be gorging on bloody bits of flesh, though the grisly morsels turned out to be only shreds of the car's red upholstery. The windows were closed, and in my ignorance, assuming their olfactory organ to be as keen as a bear's, I supposed the owner had left cold cuts in a cooler and was astonished to think they could have pecked through the roof as easily as a chick liberates itself from the egg. On the lake a boat was gliding toward shore, and as I watched, the occupant leapt to his feet, screaming, "My car! My car! Get off my car, you damn buzzards!" and promptly fell into the lake.

Yet in my photographs the unbroken shell of blue-gray metal reflects the vultures' silvery talons like still water. A few years later a chatty ranger at the Everglades Anhinga Trail told me that Ford had used fish oil in the sealants on the 1999 Taurus. The occasion for our conversation was the unusual number of black vultures on the trail, brought to the ground by the cool weather. He had just come from the parking lot, where on such days he had seen flocks of black vultures attack the sealant so vigorously that tourists returned to their cars to find the windshields popped out; he had been checking the lot for damage. True, the black, which prefers coastal areas, often dines on fish. At the Wild Bird Center on Key Largo I have watched it eat its sardine more delicately than my dog eats his meat and kibble. Once at the Anhinga Trail my husband, son, and I all observed a black vulture attending a great blue heron that had caught a fish too large for it to swallow. The heron tried it headfirst, then tail first, and sideways, dropping the fish to the ground after each attempt and walking a few steps away as if to consider another approach, but the vulture moved in to feed only after the heron gave up and departed. Perhaps its patience was only caution, for the same ranger regaled me with the tale of a photographer who got too close to a great blue, which drove its beak into the man's skull and killed him. "Most aggressive bird there is," he observed of the heron. Who can say whether a vulture is fearful or forbearing? In Darwin's era, vultures liked to tear the leather from ship's rigging, though the leather would have borne no more visual resemblance to a cow than Ford's sealant to a gar. They may be prudent, but if it's true that the blacks have no sense of smell they are not just scavengers but vandals.

———

MY FATHER LOVED CARS, though he never drove anything fancier than a Ford Crown Victoria. Mechanical though he was, a noise beneath the hood sent him into a panic. A dent or a scratch drove him wild. In the empty parking lot where the single driving lesson he gave me took place, he was so afraid I would hit something that I didn't learn to drive for another ten years. Many years after that, when I had failed to sell a new novel and had to buy a used car instead of a new one, I asked my father's advice. To my astonishment he sent me a check for five thousand dollars. I think all he ever really wanted was for me to ask his opinion on something that mattered to him. He didn't care if I told him I loved him, but he wanted that token of respect.

———

PROPERLY SPEAKING, we should not call them buzzards, buzzard being a British designation for a large hawk. The word comes from the French *busard*, which means hawk, and in the Old World *busard* refers to the genus of soaring hawks called *Buteo*, the most common of which in North America is the familiar red-tailed hawk; in Australia the bird called a black-breasted buzzard is a hawk of the genus *Hamirostra*. But we do not speak properly; in common American usage a buzzard is the same thing as a vulture; it is a contemptible, cantankerous old person; it is a greedy and ruthless person who preys upon others. As an adjective in the past it was used to mean senseless or stupid. A search of books on Amazon brings up 342 results for vultures and 363 for buzzards, including one titled *The Old Buzzard Had It Coming*.

———

ONCE I CAME ACROSS a lone black vulture feeding at the side of the road from Florida City to Convoy Point in Biscayne National Park. When I slowed the car to watch, it paused and looked up, standing over the carcass and watching me until I drove on. An hour or so later, when I drove back the same way, there was no evidence that it had ever been there. Perhaps it dragged the skeleton into the brush the moment I was out of sight. I imagine it glancing back as it carries the corpse in its mouth like my dog bearing a stick he knows I plan to confiscate. It could not carry its prize off through the air like an eagle, for though its talons are as fearsome in appearance as the eagle's, their grasp is weak. Only the bearded vulture uses its talons to grip

———

AT THE TABLE, my parents, my brother, and I often sat with our heads bowed. It was not to pray. We were trying not to talk. My parents didn't seem to remember how to have a conversation, though once, surely, they had been able to talk without erupting, had been able to speak without a fight. My father had so many allergies he didn't enjoy eating anyway. We picked at our food and waited for the meal to be over.

———

GENERALLY THE BLACK IS a communal feeder. In the rain
forest the turkey vulture is most likely to locate a kill, but at a
larger carcass it yields to the black, and both yield to the king.
Even among its own ranks the turkey is a hierarchical diner,
but feeding is less a competition than collaboration, with each
species dining on a different part of the animal. When larger
vultures tear into mammals the size of horses or cows, they
make the flesh available to the turkey, which has the weak-
est beak and on its own must content itself with animals the
size of chipmunks and squirrels. The long necks of the largest
vultures allow them to reach into the organs, while others feast
on skin, tendons, and the tougher meat. The turkey, black, and
hooded species take the scraps and pick the bones clean. In its
habitat the bearded, the only vulture to have a feathered head,
is the last to feed, for its specialty is bones, which it picks up
with its feet, swooping down to crack them against a rock. It
is reputed to prepare tortoises the same way, and the ancient
Greeks blamed it for the death of Aeschylus. As the story goes,
a bearded vulture with a tortoise in its talons mistook his bald
head for a rock and dropped the tortoise, cracking the poet's
skull. I like the irony, but the image that enchants me is that of
the feeding chimango, the caracara that Darwin observed to be
the last to leave the table, lingering at the carcass so long that
it might often be "seen within the ribs of a cow or a horse like
a bird in a cage." I picture the cathedral arch of those bleached
white ribs, inside a dark canary without song.

———

THE TURKEY VULTURE is more solitary and less aggressive
than the black. While the black defends itself by vomiting,
as a friend who shot one with an air rifle as a child learned
firsthand, the turkey more often plays dead. At the Carolina
Raptor Center, which stages a photo shoot every spring, I have

been close enough to touch it, though I would not. The bird's very solitariness precludes it.

To see a turkey vulture up close is to know the bird's tragic beauty, for there is a majesty to the crimson head, bare save for a sparse black stubble; the bird looks less bald than vulnerable and shorn, a Nazi collaborator exposed before a French village. The raised nostrils have no internal division; they are like the space left by a handle, the eye of a bloody needle of bone. All the vilification and fear the vulture inspires seem contained in the sidelong wary sadness of the eye, not the sharp black stare of an eagle or a heron's mean pupil in its fixed yellow ring, but a doleful attention that is the same soft shade of brown as my dog's. The bird's muteness sits upon its shoulders. It knows what death tastes like, but cannot speak of the flavor. To see a turkey vulture up close is to be reminded of death not as portent but as the weight of an unbearable witness. His dirge has no throat, his wisdom no voice. Two million years of silence haunt his expression. To see a turkey vulture up close is to know what loneliness looks like.

———

WHEN MY FATHER WAS YOUNG he did some hunting. When I was young he liked to fish. But he was not the kind of man who took up hobbies. He had friends, but no close ones. I don't think he ever had a pet. He filled his time by fixing things, so many things it seems now as if he must have thought everything we owned was broken.

———

IN THE UNITED STATES it is illegal not only to shoot a vulture but also to keep one as a pet. I would think few people want one, though the sister of a former president of Ecuador kept a condor, and wildlife rehabilitators report that vultures

are intelligent, more so than other raptors, as well as mischie-
vous and inquisitive. Darwin claimed that they stole a pocket
compass in a red morocco case and carried off a big black
hat. At the Carolina Raptor Center one developed a habit of
untying the staff members' shoestrings; when they tried to
trick it by wearing shoes with Velcro tabs, the bird learned
to undo those too. I think of George the Goose, who used to
unlace my boots at the train station in Princeton Junction the
year I lived in New Jersey. Or my dog, who loved to steal socks
and make us chase him through the house when he was a pup,
who greets me every morning by dropping a tennis ball on my
face. Like crows, which I have often observed skating across
the frozen surface of my backyard pond, vultures frolic. Young
blacks toss rocks like balls. They play tag and follow-the-
leader. According to the Turkey Vulture Society, some of their
soaring and circling may be for fun, just as Darwin suspected.
Their lives seemed so pleasurable to Edward Abbey—"floating
among the clouds all day, seldom stirring a feather"—that he
insisted he wanted to be reincarnated as one. They're not just
personable birds, they're sweet, insists the Society's president.
Vultures raised by humans love and trust them; even after
rejoining their natural communities they continue to respond
to human attention. One is reported to have followed a boy to
his school bus each day, flying off to forage only after the bus
was gone, and returning in the afternoon to accompany the
boy home. Only my dog comes close to being that loyal.

MY FATHER WAS A MISOGYNIST, a deeply conservative man
who felt women should be seen and not heard. He detested
women drivers and did not see the point of sending me to
college. The whole problem with his marriage, as he saw it, was
that my mother didn't want to follow; a marriage, he said, can't

have two leaders. Still he always claimed that he would not be there for her if she ever got sick—in that case, he seemed to believe, it was everyone for herself.

———

THOUGH WE THINK OF the Grim Reaper as male, in most vultures it is not possible to tell the difference between male and female by appearance, and in Federico Garcia Lorca's *Blood Wedding*, the figure of death is not a vulture itself but a beggar woman in a vulture costume. The ancient Egyptians believed that only female vultures existed; they were able to perpetuate the species because they were impregnated by the south and southeastern winds. The Egyptian goddesses Nekhbet and Mut wore vulture headdresses. Nekhbet, goddess of Upper Egypt, often portrayed as a vulture hovering at the Pharaoh's head, was also the goddess of childbirth; the hieroglyph for Mut, whom the Greeks associated with Hera, meant mother. The crown of Upper Egypt bore the image of a vulture, and the gold face mask of King Tut has a vulture over the right eye and a cobra, symbol of Lower Egypt, over the left. So sacred was the bird to the Egyptians that "Pharaoh's chicken" is the first wild animal known to have been given legal protection.

In some versions of Mayan legend the vulture is the mother and protector of the Serpent Priestess, who lived among jaguars, though in other versions the bird is male, perhaps in reference to the king vulture, whose scientific name, *Sarcorhamphus papa*, means the Pope's fleshy beak and refers to the bulb of bright orange skin above the orange and black beak. The common name predates the Spanish conquest of South America. A royal tomb dating from 450 A.D. in the pre-Colombian city of La Milpa in Belize contains the remains of a ruler known as Bird Jaguar whose adornments include a large pendant of a king vulture's head carved from jade. In Mayan legend humans descended from jaguars; the vulture, who was personified as a lord or king, was the messenger who mediated between humans and the gods, "the conduit to the gods and the afterworld...deified and venerated as an ancestor and god after his death."

Some Indian villages in Peru have annual ceremonies involving the condor. One re-enacts the Spanish conquest and Quechua myth by pairing a bull, introduced to Peru by the Spanish, with a native condor, whose feet are sewn to the back of the bull with strips of leather. In frenzy the two creatures buck, pitch, and lurch around the plaza together. If the condor survives it is released, a victory that symbolizes successful Indian resistance, though I can't help wondering how the Indians overcome the resistance of bird and beast to the process of the sewing.

The Andean condor, which appeared on the pottery and textiles of cultures that predate the Incas, is still a symbol of strength and endurance in South America, figuring on the national crests of Bolivia, Chile, Columbia, and Ecuador. In Chile the condor is a coin featuring the bird's image. The name of Chile's capital province, Cundinamarca, comes from the native word for condor, and in Bolivia the Order of the Condor is the highest award of merit.

In North America we know the California condor as the Thunderbird through the legends of the Tlingit, who believed the flapping of its wings to cause thunder and lightning to flash from its eyes. In many West Coast native communities shamans were believed to receive their powers from the condor. The Costanoans raised raptors to be sacrificed at funerals, eagles to Venus and condors to Mars. In Iroquois legend the Golden Eagle, Head Chief of all the birds, chose vultures as his faithful servants, for it was his law that the earth be kept clean.

In African folklore the bird's ability to show up wherever there is a carcass is a sign of extrasensory powers, though not all myths venerate vultures. In Hindu belief, vultures are carriers of the human spirit but also the gatekeepers of hell. In European folklore the bearded vulture has a reputation as predatory as that of the wolf, though its otherworldliness makes it more frightening. In North American Tsimshian legends the condor abducts young women and destroys its rivals with a great wind. And in ancient Greek myth, it was not two eagles but two bearded vultures that flew down to tear out Prometheus's liver every day. Whether they were male or female legend does not say.

———

MY FATHER WAS NOT a religious man. As a child he was sent to Catholic schools, where a nun rapped his hand with a metal-edged ruler and split his knuckles. Did he look up, I wonder, when he felt the chill of her shadow, or did he just hear the sweeping wing of the nun's black habit as she brought the blade of the ruler down? I don't know if he had any faith before. He never did after. His view of death was practical, his view of life dark. He threatened to die so often it was a shock when he did.

———

BOTH TIBETANS AND THE PARSEES of India dispose of their dead by feeding them to vultures. According to myth Shakyamuni Buddha gave himself to feed a hungry tiger; in another version he fed his own flesh to a hawk in order to spare a pigeon—thus sky burial is regarded as a final act of charity in which the deceased provides food to sustain living things, and the Tibetan name for the practice, *jhator*, means giving alms to the birds. Interference with *jhator* is a serious breach of Tibetan religion, in which the vultures, sacred messengers called *Dakinis*, the Tibetan equivalent of angels, are believed to carry the soul up to heaven, where it will await reincarnation. Tibetans fear they will not return if driven away. In Xue Xinran's nonfiction account of a Chinese woman's search for her soldier husband in Tibet, the Tibetans were so angry at the Chinese solder, who accidentally disrupted a wartime sky burial by shooting one of the vultures, he could placate them only by killing himself, allowing the Tibetans to call back the sacred birds by feeding them his flesh.

Although *jhator* is embedded in Tibetan Buddhism, its origins predate the religion in Tibet. The kings of the Yarlung dynasty were entombed and the remains of Dalai Lamas and other high Buddhist figures are preserved in stupas or encased in gold, but neither burial nor cremation is practical in a country with so little fuel and such hard ground. Until Buddhism was introduced in the ninth century water burial was the most common method of disposal—poor people simply dropped the bodies of their dead into a river, though in more elaborate forms of water burial the corpse was cut into small pieces to be consumed by fish, just as it is dismembered and hacked into pieces for the vultures in *jhator*, which is now chosen by more than three-quarters of Tibetans. Those who cannot afford the *o-yogin* butcher simply place their dead on high rocks for the birds and wild dogs.

At the Drigung Monastery in csentral Tibet, best known of the three major sites, as many as ten sky burials are conducted a day. Here the vultures are so sated they must be coaxed to eat, but at many of the more remote sites the birds are so ravenous they must be fended off with sticks while the body is prepared. Though it is considered a bad omen if they do not consume the entire corpse, a sign that demons have taken over the spirit, some remote sites are strewn with tufts of hair and bones, as well as scraps of clothing, beer bottles, broken axe handles, and rusty blades. At Langmusi on the Sichuan border, where tickets to the *jhator* illustrated with a flock of vultures devouring a human body are sold despite the efforts of the Chinese to restrict attendance, one witness reports seeing a headless, armless skeleton.

At such remote sites the ceremony may be no more than a prayer uttered by the single butcher, but at Drigung preparations begin the day before, when the body is washed, shaved, placed in a fetal position, and wrapped in a white shroud. Lamas chanting prayers to release the soul from purgatory lead the procession to the charnel ground, a large fenced meadow with a circle of stones surrounded by prayer flags. At dawn the sky burial master blows a horn and lights a fire of juniper or mulberry branches to summon the vultures to roll out a five-colored road between heaven and earth, though surely the incense also helps purify the foul air. While the mourners watch, the *o-yogin* butcher or *tomden* rips off the shroud and begins the dismemberment, cajoling the vultures as he hacks off limbs, removes the flesh and smashes the bones. Often he and his assistants laugh and chat as they work, mixing the pulverized bones with a *tsampa* of roasted barley flour, yak butter, and tea to make them more palatable to the birds. All the while they speak to the vultures, coaxing, inviting.

"Eat, eat," they say in Tibetan, "*Shey, shey.*" "Birdies," they call in a language that seems less their own than the birds'.

In India, where the actual consumption of the body is hidden from view, sky burials are required by orthodox Parsee doctrine, which holds that corpses contaminate anything they touch and therefore cannot be buried, cremated, or thrown in the river. Here the body is placed in a closed granite structure with one-hundred foot towers known as the *dakhma*. Once all clothing and adornment have been removed with hooked rods and the body has been washed, perfumed with myrrh, and blessed by the officiating priest, it is placed on one of the three-tiered stones atop the towers, open at the top to the vultures. When the body is ready, a signal is given, and male mourners in a nearby prayer pavilion begin praying. It is the voice of their prayers that summons the birds.

—

THERE WAS NO SERVICE for my father; he wanted none. No prayers, no eulogies. He would have liked a brief notice of his death in the newsletter put out by Texaco, the company for which he had worked for forty years, but his companion was afraid for strangers to know she was alone, and so he had no obituary either. Only a death certificate marked his passing. His body was cremated, his ashes scattered from a plane over the Gulf of Mexico.

Years later, in a restaurant where I had taken her to lunch, my mother said, out of the blue, "I think it's good what your father did. Potassium for the fish."

I was so upset—we were *eating*; we hadn't been talking about my father, except for the running conversation in her head—I dropped my fork and went to the ladies' room and wept. When she came in a few minutes later it was to rinse her partial plate.

"You don't know how lucky you are," she said. "You still have all your teeth. You can eat whatever you want."

My father was who he was. He died how he died. But because he was my father I loved him.

—

THOUGH IT SEEMS AS IF the symbol of death ought to be eternal, vultures, slow breeders who eat at the top of the food chain, are particularly vulnerable to environmental threats. What will we fear if the buzzard is gone? In the United States though populations of black and turkey vultures are increasing thanks to our bounty of roadkill, a captive breeding program was necessary to save the California condor, which came so close to extinction that by 1987 there were only three birds left in the wild. It will take more than that to save the Old World vultures of South Asia, the long-billed griffon, slender-billed, and Indian white-backed vultures, all listed as Critically Endangered, the highest level of risk for extinction, by the World Conservation Union.

So radically has the vulture population of South Asia declined that in 2001 the Parsee Council of India installed solar reflectors to speed decomposition in the dakhma, where more than a hundred vultures are needed to keep up with the three or four corpses a day. It is not just the Parsees who are affected by their disappearance. We may loathe vultures, but we need them.

Carcasses of animals that the vultures are no longer numerous enough to consume have created public health problems in Pakistan, India, and Nepal. Besides the diseases spread by the carcasses themselves, rotting carrion has resulted in a booming population of feral dogs and outbreaks of rabies. In Europe the vulture population is one percent of what it was in the nineteenth century. We may have learned the lesson of DDT, but only recently has the decline of the vulture population in Asia been traced to Diclofenac. An anti-inflammatory used to treat sick cattle, it causes renal failure in vultures and is so lethal that contamination of less than one percent of livestock carcasses created the most rapid population decline ever recorded for a wild bird. Perhaps the recent ban will save them, though it's too soon to know whether anything can keep them from going the way of the dinosaurs and woolly mammoths.

—

MY FATHER LEFT NO NOTE, of course. I wouldn't have
expected one, though I looked.

———

WHEN VULTURES WOO they seem to summon all the voice
their unequipped throats can muster. The New World black
spreads his wings, lowers his head and emits a puffing sound;
the turkey groans. It is as close to a serenade as these creatures
without song can come. When they warn they grunt or hiss;
they may even snarl. But what I hear does not sound like a
grunt or a hiss, nor croaking coo nor snarl, not a puffing or
a groan; it is more a low, embryonic woofing, not the voice
itself but the anticipation of one reverberating deep inside the
throat. I cannot tell whether they are warning me or wooing,
though here in their midst, surrounded by a flock of them at
the edge of an empty parking lot in the Everglades, it would
seem important to know.

In the end they ignore me. They wander off; I pack up my
camera and tripod and go. I will learn their habits and more,
but I will never speak their language.

Yet some of the happiest hours of my life have been spent in
the open air of a salt marsh in the company of birds. It is an
acquired taste, for I grew up in the Midwest, where farmland
falls away from the road like a low tide and the highway seems
an endless bridge over nothing, the horizon so treeless and
vast that if someone beside a farmhouse a mile away lifted a
hand to wave I would see it. The Midwest affords everyone a
vulture's view. Perhaps that is why it has always seemed such a
lonely place to me. Even in the safety of my car I feel dwarfed
and exposed.

If I ever saw vultures wheeling in the sky over the Midwestern
cornfields I don't remember. The first time I saw one on the
ground was at Merritt Island National Wildlife Refuge in

Florida. My father had died less than two months before, and
I was on my way home from his house, the house that I now
owned, where I had spent the past week working on his estate.
I knew of the Refuge only from a picture on a calendar; it was
not a place I had always longed to see, but a place that was
on my way home. Stopping was an attempt to give that dark
errand some small facet of pleasure.

Driving the highway through the Everglades to Flamingo,
I always feel on the edge of openness in the way I am on the
edge of it as I pass over the Midwestern farmland, a traveler, an
observer, a person apart. It is different at Merritt Island, where
an unpaved road winds along dikes once used for mosquito
control, a sandy seven-mile lane through one hundred forty
thousand acres of saltwater estuaries, brackish marsh, and
freshwater lagoons. I rarely saw another car in the two days
I spent cruising the wildlife drive and paved back road, radio
off, windows and sunroof open, eating peanut butter crackers
for lunch and peeing in a Dixie cup I dumped out the window.
In the afternoon I walked the trails through the hammocks of
oak and palm, listening to the drill of a pileated woodpecker
whose bright red crest I could just spot through the trees.
At dawn I parked beside the swales where egrets, ibises, and
wood storks fed and squabbled. Each time I opened my door
they flushed upward with a great whooshing of wings, then
settled again like parachutes, pecking and squawking. On the
ponds there were great black formations of coots, and in the
distance a streamer of dazzling white pelicans. In the clarity of the weak winter light the mudflats glittered, quivering
with sandpipers and tiny crustaceans, while an osprey sailed
the far sky. A rail skittered into the brush at the start of the
Cruickshank Trail, the five-mile loop I hiked around a shallow
lagoon and through the marsh while a balmy breeze wisped
at my collar and fingered my hair. The only sound was the

whistling *kik–kik–kik* of the terns that swooped and dipped
and flashed their forked white origami tails against the bright
blue heaven. I had not spoken a word for two days. The landscape was as wide, as exposed and dwarfing as the Midwest,
but I had disappeared inside it. When I got back to my car,
four turkey vultures blocked the narrow road. They were huge,
rough feathered, dark, a color I would describe as more a dirty
chocolate than black; the sun shone off the red heads and
ivory hooks of their beaks. Though I confess to superstition,
they did not strike me as an omen. Despite the recentness of
grief they did not remind me of death or its tedious business.
They were simply there, as I was, in a kind of matter-of-factness so profound we can know it only in nature. It may have
been a minute or ten that we regarded one another. Then they
waddled to the side and let me pass. That evening, driving
the back road, I came upon a vulture tree. It was dusk, and
the hunkering vultures and bare black bones of the branches
were silhouetted against the faded dust-blue sky in a way that
seemed incredibly beautiful to me. It is in such confrontations
with the eternal shape of death that we know most fully we're
alive.

In "The Snows of Kilimanjaro" the dying writer dreams that
he is saved, carried by a small silver plane up over the wilde-
beest and zebras, the forests and bamboo slopes, only to understand that where he is going is into the unbelievable whiteness
of death. He is borne on the buzzard's wing, like a Buddhist
carried up to heaven by the *dakhini*.

I do not dream of vultures. I have never dreamed of flying,
though as a child, lying in the dark, awake, voiceless, listening
to my parents fight, I used to dream of escape. Perhaps that's
why I grew up to be a writer. In bed at night now my dog
nests against my thigh. Sometimes in his sleep he twitches
and yips, chasing squirrels, tasting the hunt. Africans believe

that vultures dream the location of their food. But who really knows where the dog and vulture soar while they sleep? Why would we dream never to leave the domain of our waking world? I don't know where I go as I sink into the blackness of that temporary death, only that in the morning I wake with a low woofing in my throat that, if I'm lucky, will turn into song.

PUBLICATION NOTES

EARLIER VERSIONS OF SOME of these essays appeared in the following journals and are gratefully reprinted with permission: "In the Garden of the Word," *Antaeus* 59; "The End of the Counterculture," *Southern Quarterly* 34; "A House in Florida," *Five Points* Volume 6, Number 1; "A Stone's Weight," *Shenandoah* Volume 55, Number 1; "A Grand Canyon," *Prairie Schooner* Volume 83, Number 1; "Black Widow," *storySouth* 27; "Mud Pies," *Michigan Quarterly Review* Volume XLV, Number 3; "Morning Light," *Crab Orchard Review* Volume 12, Number 1; "Geography for Writers," *North Carolina Literary Review* 17, and "Buzzards," *Southern Humanities Review* Volume 41, Number 2. "Buzzards" was reprinted in *The Best American Essays 2008*, and a portion of "Morning Light" also appeared under the title "Morning Light, Ocracoke Island" in *Southern Humanities Review* Volume 37, Number 3.

Acknowledgments

—

I THANK *Southern Humanities Review* for the Theodore
Christian Hoepfner Award for "Buzzards," *Prairie Schooner* for
a Glenna Luschei Award for "A Grand Canyon," and Robert
Atwan of *The Best American Essays* for the many notable essay
citations.

I would also like to thank the North Carolina Arts
Council for a fellowship grant in nonfiction, the Blumenthal
Foundation and Wildacres Retreat for offering a place to work,
to be inspired, and to gather with so many other artists, and
the writers who read early drafts of these essays and offered
their invaluable suggestions: Jim Clark, Michael Gaspeny,
Craig Nova, Michael Parker, Dave Shaw, and Jill Storey. My
thanks also to Meg Reid for her editorial wisdom and design.
I am extremely grateful to Betsy Teter and John Lane of the
Hub City Writers Project. All writers owe Betsy, John, and
Hub City a huge hurrah for making such beautiful books and
helping to keep literature alive. And my utmost thanks always
to my family, Michael, Max, and Al.

HUB CITY
PRESS

HUB CITY PRESS is a non-profit independent press in Spartanburg, SC, that publishes well-crafted, high-quality works by new and established authors, with an emphasis on the Southern experience. We are committed to high-caliber novels, short stories, poetry, plays, memoir, and works emphasizing regional culture and history. We are particularly interested in books with a strong sense of place.

Hub City Press is an imprint of the non-profit Hub City Writers Project, founded in 1995 to foster a sense of community through the literary arts. Our metaphor of organization purposely looks backward to the nineteenth century when Spartanburg was known as the "hub city," a place where railroads converged and departed.

RECENT HUB CITY PRESS TITLES

In the Garden of Stone • Susan Tekulve

Voodoo for the Other Woman • Angela Kelly

Literary Dogs • John Lane and Betsy Wakefield Teter

The Iguana Tree • Michel Stone

Patron Saint of Dreams • Philip Gerard

Waking • Ron Rash